D1259283

THE SCHOLARSHIP OF WILLIAM FOXWELL ALBRIGHT

HARVARD SEMITIC MUSEUM

HARVARD SEMITIC STUDIES

Frank Moore Cross, editor

THE SCHOLARSHIP OF WILLIAM FOXWELL ALBRIGHT
An Appraisal

Papers Delivered at the Symposium
"Homage to William Foxwell Albright"

The American Friends of the Israel Exploration Society

Rockville, Maryland, 1984

Edited by
Gus W. Van Beek

With Contributions by:

Frank Moore Cross, Jr.
David Noel Freedman
Delbert R. Hillers
Gus W. Van Beek

Scholars Press
Atlanta, Georgia

THE SCHOLARSHIP OF WILLIAM FOXWELL ALBRIGHT

by
Gus Van Beek

© 1989
The President and Fellows of Harvard College

Library of Congress Cataloging in Publication Data

The Scholarship of William Foxwell Albright: an appraisal/Gus Van Beek
p. cm. -- (Harvard Semitic studies; no. 33)
Proceedings of a symposium held Oct. 21, 1984 in honor of William
Foxwell Albright.
ISBN 1-55540-314-X
1. Albright, William Foxwell, 1891-1971--Congresses
2. Semitists--United States--Biography--Congresses.
3. Archaeologists--United States--Biography--Congresses.
I. Albright, William Foxwell, 1891-1971. II. Van Beek, Gus W. (Gus Willard), 1922- III. Series
PJ30009.A43S36   1989   88-37334
950'.07204--dc19   CIP

Printed in the United States of America
on acid-free paper

Table of Contents

Homage to William Foxwell Albright

Preface

Benjamin Adelman

The idea for a symposium on William Foxwell Albright was really initiated by Governor Harry Hughes of Maryland when he approved a resolution officially declaring 1984 as the year for commemorating the 350th anniversary of Maryland's founding in 1634. Later, we received a copy of "Artscapes," the newsletter of the Montgomery County Arts Council, which contained an article on planning Maryland's 350th birthday celebration, and inviting Maryland organizations to participate.

This was highly desirable because it encouraged public interest in history. But how could it possibly relate to the American Friends of the Israel Exploration Society (AFIES)? We soon realized that Albright, who had figured so prominently in studies relating to the land that is now Israel, was indeed a Marylander; he had spent almost his entire adult life in the State, and he had raised the Johns Hopkins University to worldwide eminence in the field of Ancient Near Eastern studies. A 1984 celebration of Albright's achievements sponsored by the Society would be most appropriate.

What form should this AFIES event take? Albright deserved more than a single lecture. He was not a narrow specialist; over the years, he had made significant contributions to a wide range of fields. A symposium would be more suitable. Who should be invited to speak about these contributions? Fortunately, we knew Gus W. Van Beek, who had been one of Albright's students, and had lectured to our society several times. I called him and discussed the project. He liked the idea and agreed to serve as chairman of the symposium. He accepted the responsibility for selecting scholars to participate in the symposium, while the AFIES agreed to take care of the operating details. The symposium, entitled "Homage to William Foxwell Albright," would feature a series of lectures by Albright's pupils, each of whom would discuss an aspect of Albright's contribution to ancient Near Eastern studies, interspersed with two unstructured panel discussions and two question-and-answer sessions dealing with Albright as a scholar, teacher, and friend. We presented these plans to the the staff of the Jewish Community Center of Greater Washington, and found everyone enthusiastic. It could be held on a Sunday afternoon and evening when a maximum number of people might attend, and Sunday, October 21, 1984, was scheduled for the event. A planning committee was set up, including Van Beek, a representative of the Center, and members of the AFIES board. Then we went to work.

It soon became evident that even with the Center's cooperation, additional support would be needed. The society, therefore, applied to the Maryland-Humanities Council for a grant. The application was approved in due course, with the Council making several useful recommendations.

We wish to thank the Maryland Humanities Council for its assistance that made the symposium possible. We also wish to acknowledge with deep gratitude the efforts of the staff of the Jewish Community Center of Greater Washington as well as many AFIES members to make the event a success; when the day of the symposium came, everything went smoothly.

It should also be mentioned that Gus Van Beek proposed that the proceedings of the symposium should be published. He has served as the editor, and this book is the result.

Since AFIES was founded several years after Albright had passed away, we never had the good fortune to have him lecture to our society. Albright was not an "ivory tower" scholar; he liked to share his knowledge with interested audiences such as ours. This book is a means to that end.

The Organization of the Symposium

Gus W. Van Beek

Smithsonian Institution

From the first planning meeting for the Symposium, it was agreed that the theme should focus on W. F. Albright's contributions to Near Eastern studies, a field embodying a number of diverse and interrelated disciplines and sub-disciplines. During his lifetime, a prodigious burst of archaeological fieldwork and chance discoveries in the Fertile Crescent and the Eastern Mediterranean occurred, yielding a flood of new information that revolutionized established disciplines, and created new areas of specialization. Endowed with a first-rate mind, a photographic memory, a full measure of what he called "disciplined intuition" and common sense, and an interest in the integration of specialized parts into a coherent whole, Albright eagerly participated in this research. He contributed significantly to a host of disciplines and sub-disciplines, and developed as complete a synthesis as possible, which was beyond the scope of any of his contemporaries and his students.

We recognized that this synthesis could not be adequately evaluated in the Symposium. On the other hand, to deal primarily with his contributions to specific areas, e.g., to Ugaritic studies, to Hebrew poetry, to proto-Sinaitic inscriptions, would obscure Albright's impact on the entire spectrum of Near Eastern studies. The obvious choice was to organize the Symposium around his contributions to major disciplines within the field: Epigraphy, Philology, History, Biblical Studies, and Archaeology. Even so, a number of major areas of Near Eastern studies, such as Historical Geography, Chronology, Assyriology, and Egyptology, to which made substantial contributions, could not be included within the time frame of a one-day symposium. Nevertheless, allusions to and discussions of contributions to these disciplines and sub-disciplines appear throughout the papers because of the interrelatedness of the field of study as a whole. I hope these will remind readers of the astonishing breadth of this generalist.

It was further agreed that the Symposium should critically examine Albright's contributions to these disciplines. For Albright, homage without honest appraisal would have been little more than flattery, and therefore without merit. Throughout his life, he seized on new discoveries and developments that filled gaps, corrected mistakes, altered equations, and overturned interpretations. Indeed, it has been repeatedly noted, not always with sympathetic understanding, that Albright often changed his mind. These shifts of position resulted from the integration of new material into his frame of reference. Furthermore, during the 13 years between his death and this

3

Symposium, vast quantities of new material emerged that overturned or modified earlier assumptions.   Not all of the new data fully supported Albright's reconstructions. The Symposium should, therefore, examine the degree to which his work is standing the test of time.

We also decided to select the Symposium participants from among Albright's students whose scholarly careers had focused on different areas of specialization within the larger field of Near Eastern studies. His students were acquainted with the many facets of his interests, the workings of his mind, and the patterns of his oral and written expression. The task, then, involved choosing representative pupils to evaluate his contributions to the major disciplines. The final selection included:

Epigraphy:	Frank Moore Cross, Jr.	Hancock Professor of Hebrew and other Oriental Languages, Harvard University.
History:	David Noel Freedman	Arthur F. Thurnau Professor of Biblical Studies, and Director, Program of Studies in Religion, University of Michigan.
Philology:	Delbert R. Hillers	W.W. Spence Professor of Semitic Languages, the Johns Hopkins University.
Biblical Studies:	Samuel Iwry	Distinguished Professor of Hebrew Literature, Baltimore Hebrew College, Professor of Near Eastern Eastern Studies, the Johns Hopkins University.
Archaeology:	Gus W. Van Beek	Curator, Old World Archaeology, Smithsonian Institution.

As Mr. Adelman has noted in the Preface, the Symposium -- "Homage to William Foxwell Albright" -- was held in the Jewish Community Center of Greater Washington, October 21, 1984, during the afternoon and evening. The schedule included: An opening panel discussion by the five speakers on the subject, "Albright as Seen by His Students." Thereafter, the first two papers--by Cross and Hillers--were read, followed by the first question-and-answer session. Van Beek and Freedman presented their papers next, after which the Symposium adjourned for dinner. After dinner, the meeting resumed with Iwry reading his paper, followed by the second panel discussion of the participants on the topic, "The Present Status of Albright's Contributions and the Future of These Fields." A final question-and-answer session closed the meeting. The entire proceedings were recorded on audio-cassettes and subsequently transcribed.

Before Hillers presented his paper, he made the following announcement: "Good afternoon. Dr. Van Beek has allowed me before the reading of my paper to make an announcement. Some of you may know this, but for all of us I think it will nevertheless be a happy announcement, that through the generosity of Harvey Meyerhoff and Lynn Meyerhoff of Baltimore, a chair named after Professor Albright has been established at the Johns Hopkins University. This is the William Foxwell Albright Chair of Biblical and Near Eastern Studies. And their munificent gift assures us that something of the spirit of Professor Albright will continue on through decades to come. Our only problem now will be to find someone like Professor Albright to fill it." Since the Symposium, that Chair has been happily filled by P. Kyle McCarter, Jr.

In this publication, the papers appear in alphabetical order by author. Unfortunately, Dr. Iwry was unable to finish his manuscript for publication, and we regret its omission. A short biography of Albright's life has been included, primarily for lay persons without easy access to journals and books, to provide a chronological framework for the contributions discussed here, and to help explain aspects of his character, habits, and methods that may aid in understanding this great scholar. In writing this biography, the author depended heavily on the following sources: the major Albright biography by Leona Running and David Noel Freedman, *William Foxwell Albright* (Two Continents Publishing Group, New York, 1975); an obituary by Freedman, "William Foxwell Albright: In Memoriam," *Bulletin of the American Schools of Oriental Research* 205 (1972) pp. 3-13; a tribute by Frank Moore Cross, Jr. "William Foxwell Albright: Orientalist," *Bulletin of the American Schools of Oriental Research* 200 (1970) pp. 7-11; and a list of the Ph.D. dissertation titles of Albright's students published by Freedman, *The Published Works of William Foxwell Albright: A Comprehensive Bibliography* (American Schools of Oriental Research, Cambridge, 1975). He also made full use of his own recollections based on a close association with Albright while a student and research associate in the Oriental Seminary, 1946-1947 and especially 1949--1959.

William Foxwell Albright: A Short Biography

Gus W. Van Beek

Smithsonian Institution

William Foxwell (né Thomas) Albright was born May 24, 1891, to Wilbur Finley and Zephine Viola Foxwell Albright in Coquimbo, Chile. Descended from English and German farmers in northern Iowa, his devout Methodist parents served as missionaries in Chile after a brief parish ministry. William and his five younger brothers and sisters received most of their primary education from their mother. As a boy, he read widely in his father's library, pursuing his own emerging interests in ancient history and religion and, at the age of 10, he purchased Rogers, *History of Babylonia and Assyria* with money he had saved. His natural inclination toward intellectual pursuits may have been enhanced by two life-long physical disabilities: extreme myopia, perhaps caused by typhoid fever in infancy, and a deformed left hand, impaired in a rope-and-pulley accident when he was five years old. Both handicaps prevented such normal activities as sports and automobile driving throughout his lifetime; yet neither was so disabling as to preclude farm work during his youth, walking the length and breadth of Palestine, and typing faster and more accurately with his own "hunt-and-peck" system than many professional typists.

Upon returning to Iowa at the age of 12, William attended public school and eventually entered the preparatory department of Upper Iowa University. When he was 16, he began the self-study of Hebrew in his spare time. During his undergraduate years at Upper Iowa University, he studied Greek, Latin, mathematics, and the sciences, receiving his A. B. degree in 1912. The following year he became principal of a small high school in Menno, South Dakota, a predominantly German-speaking community, where he improved his German, and studied Akkadian on his own. He wrote a paper on Akkadian *Dallalu*, which was published in the *Orientalistische Literaturzeitung* at the same time that he successfully applied for a graduate fellowship to study under Paul Haupt, in the Oriental Seminary of the Johns Hopkins University.

At Hopkins, Albright's studies centered on languages and literatures: Hebrew, Akkadian, Egyptian, Ethiopic, Syriac, and Arabic, an emphasis that he would later require of his students. He held the Rayner Fellowship for three years, and received his Ph.D. in 1916, with a dissertation entitled, "The Assyrian Deluge Epic," which was never published. Albright received the Thayer Fellowship of the American Schools of Oriental Research, Jerusalem, in 1916, but had to defer acceptance because of World War I.

7

During the next two academic years, he served as the Johnston Scholar and instructor in the Oriental Seminary teaching Akkadian and Arabic, while continuing his studies of languages and literatures, and writing papers on diverse topics. His academic career was interrupted by the military draft in 1918, in which he was called to limited service in the U.S. Army.

Late in 1919, Albright arrived in Jerusalem as the Thayer Fellow of the American Schools of Oriental Research. He immediately began studying modern Hebrew and modern Arabic, folklore, topography, and archaeology. During these early years, he made many field trips by foot, horseback, and automobile to all parts of Palestine, examining sites, collecting and dating potsherds, increasing his knowledge of the historical geography of the land and its cultural chronology. He also undertook as many journeys as possible to other countries, including Lebanon, Syria, Egypt, and Iraq (Mesopotamia). He possessed considerable physical stamina as demonstrated by his walking trips throughout Palestine that lasted days and sometimes weeks at a time, and by his frequent archaeological field work.

In 1920, he was named Acting Director of the Jerusalem School and in 1921, Director. That same year, he married Dr. Ruth Norton, a fellow student at Hopkins who had just received her Ph.D. in Sanskrit. She gave up a promising scholarly career to devote herself to her husband and eventually to their four sons, Paul, Hugh, Stephen, and David. At the same time, in his capacity as Director, he was heavily involved with plans for the new ASOR school buildings, the construction of which began in 1924 and was completed in 1925.

Albright's archaeological career began with the excavation of Tell el-Fûl in 1922 and 1923. With M. G. Kyle, he undertook the excavation of Tell Beit Mirsim in 1926, followed by three more field seasons in 1928, 1930, and 1932. The publication of this site appeared in the *Annual of the American Schools of Oriental Research*, vols. XII (1932), XIII (1933), XVII (1938), and XXI-XXII (1943).

He continued as Director of the American School of Oriental Research in Jerusalem until 1929 when he resigned to accept the W. W. Spence Chair in Semitic Languages at the Johns Hopkins University, the Chair held by Haupt until his death in 1926. His relationship with the American Schools remained strong with his appointment as Editor of the *Bulletin of the American Schools of Oriental Research (BASOR)* in 1930. This position, which he held for the next 38 years, provided an immediate outlet for his research and enabled him to exert an enormous influence in Near Eastern studies. In 1933, he accepted a continuing appointment as Director of the Jerusalem School on a half-yearly basis.

During the early 1930's, Albright resumed his program of excavations, centered as before in the hill country of Palestine. In 1931 with O. R. Sellers, he began field work at Beth-zur; in 1932, he conducted his last season at Tell Beit Mirsim; in 1933, he reinvestigated the stratigraphy of Tell el-Fûl, sections of which had been freshly exposed by the 1927 earthquake, and briefly joined excavations at Ader in Transjordan; in 1934, he initiated excavations at Bethel with J. L. Kelso, and spent two weeks of field work at the Conway High Place at Petra. Although busy with excavations, Albright found time to continue research and writing. Apart from articles, he published the Richards Lectures under the title, *The Archaeology of Palestine and the Bible* in 1932, and a monograph, *The Vocalization of the Egyptian Syllabic Orthography* in 1934.

At the end of 1935, he resigned his annual six-month directorship at the American School in Jerusalem, ending sixteen years of intimate involvement with the School and with Palestine. The Jerusalem Period had enabled Albright to master a series of interrelated disciplines, to travel the land, to dig in its mounds, and to begin the correlation of biblical, historical, geographical, archaeological, and ethnological information into a new synthesis.

Returning to Baltimore, he concentrated on scholarship, teaching, editorial work, service to learned societies, and to the academic world. He also devoted special attention to refugee scholars fleeing Nazi persecution in Europe, and was instrumental in finding academic positions in the United States for a number of distinguished colleagues, an activity motivated by his idealism and humanity.

His continuing research culminated in several major publications, chief of which, *From the Stone Age to Christianity*, appeared in 1940. In this work, he drew on all disciplines and relevant cultures to show the substantial historicity of the Bible as received and as illuminated by contemporary Near Eastern literatures and archaeological discoveries, all set in his organismic philosophy of history. This synthesis, which was uniquely Albright, eventually destroyed much of the Wellhausenian view of the unilinear evolution of culture and religion. In place of the latter, it provided a new, integrated view of the cultural history of the "Bible Lands." Incidentally, the "Bible Lands," was the name he used to indicate the territory from Gibraltar to the Indus River and from southern Russia to Ethiopia. In 1942, his *Archaeology and the Religion of Israel* was published; it contained the Ayer Foundation lectures that he had delivered the year before at the Colgate-Rochester Divinity School, with extensive reworking and numerous additions. He also wrote *The Archaeology of Palestine* for the Penguin Book Series (Pelican Books in the U.S.A.), which was published in 1949.

One of the most notable events of the post-War years occurred in 1947 with the discovery of the Dead Sea Scrolls of the Essene Community at Qumrân, near the Dead Sea. Albright was one of the first scholars to pronounce them authentic and to date them from the second century B.C. to the first century A.D. His initial determination of the date was based on two photographs sent from the American School of Oriental Research, Jerusalem by John Trever, one of the fellows of the School. For nearly a decade, Albright argued their authenticity and Hellenistic dating in a running dispute with several scholars, chiefly S. Zeitlin and G. R. Driver, who variously questioned the antiquity of the Scrolls, suggested a date as late as the Mediaeval period, or regarded them as forgeries.

Following World War II, Albright returned to archaeological field work during the winter of 1947-48. With Wendell Phillips, a young California explorer whom he had met during the War, he traveled to Egypt and Sinai, concentrating on remains in the vicinity of Serâbît el-Khâdem of the mid-second millennium B.C., where the proto-Sinaitic inscriptions had been discovered. These texts are among the earliest Semitic alphabetic inscriptions known, and this trip gave Albright his first opportunity to examine the actual inscriptions, whose decipherment occupied him from time-to-time throughout his scholarly career.

In 1949, Wendell Phillips established the American Foundation for the Study of Man (AFSM) with Albright as First Vice President; the AFSM provided the organizational structure for initiating field work in southern Arabia. During the winter of 1949-50, they began the excavation of three sites in Wadi Beihan, West Aden Protectorate (now South Yemen); they returned with a larger field party for a longer and more productive field season in 1950-51. With this campaign, Albright's career as a field archaeologist came to an end, owing chiefly to increasing commitments to research and writing, heavy demands for lecturing, and diminishing physical strength.

In 1953, Albright visited the new State of Israel, marking his first return to Palestine following his departure in 1935. He was accorded a welcome scarcely exceeded by a head of state. He lectured in Hebrew to an audience of no less than 2000 in Beer-sheva, delivered public lectures in Jerusalem, Tel Aviv, and Haifa, and was taken on several excursions to see the Negev and to visit recently excavated archaeological sites.

He served as an exchange scholar to Turkey under the State Department's Cultural Exchange Program during 1956. This provided an opportunity to visit archaeological sites and to study Hittite material first hand, in addition to meeting Turkish colleagues and lecturing.

At the end of the 1957-58 academic year, Albright retired from the Johns Hopkins University after 29 years of teaching and chairing the Oriental Seminary. His retirement years were largely given over to travel in conjunction with his service as visiting professor at a number of universities and seminaries, acceptance of many lectureships in established series, and continuing activities in national and international professional organizations. His fame made him a much sought-after lecturer by institutions concerned with religion and with the humanities, and he often delivered more than one lecture per day, sometimes in different cities. He also carried a heavy burden of correspondence with colleagues, students, and the general public.

These activities not only diverted his time and attention from research and writing, but also consumed his physical strength. From the beginning of his studies at Hopkins to the end of his life, Albright suffered episodes of illness, usually characterized by eyestrain and nervous exhaustion. These illnesses generally followed periods of intense concentrated activity, and recovery often required bedrest for several days. In the later years, the episodes became more frequent, and recuperation demanded increasingly longer periods of rest. His eyesight deteriorated even more, owing to glaucoma and the development of cataracts.

Yet he managed to continue research in a number of directions that resulted in several significant books, a host of articles, and a considerable number of unfinished manuscripts. He spent the 1958-1959 academic year as Research Professor at the Jewish Theological Seminary, New York, writing a book on the history of the religion of Israel, one in a series of volumes on Jewish religion organized by Louis Finkelstein, Chancellor of the Seminary. Regrettably the manuscript was never finished. But a number of major works were published during this period. *The Biblical Period from Abraham to Ezra* (Harper Torchbooks TB 102, New York) in 1963, provided an up-dated expansion of the first chapter of *The Jews: Their History, Culture and Religion* (1949) edited by Louis Finkelstein, based on new discoveries and Albright's maturing views of the development of Israel's institutions. This was followed in 1964 by *History, Archaeology and Christian Humanism* (London), a series of 15 previously published essays somewhat loosely organized around the themes represented in the title, and--in Chapters 14 and 15--Albright's only autobiographical material known to the writer. His most definitive publication reflecting his years of research on the Serâbît el-Khâdem texts appeared in a monograph, *The Proto-Sinaitic Inscriptions and Their Decipherment* in 1966. The Jordan lectures, which he had delivered in the University of London in 1965, were published under the title *Yahweh and the Gods of Canaan* in 1968.

In 1961 while teaching at Hebrew Union College, Albright was honored on the occasion of his 70th birthday with the presentation of a *Festschrift, The Bible and the Ancient Near East*, consisting of a collection of essays in diverse sub-disciplines, edited by G. E. Wright. Ten of the 14 articles were written by Albright's students.

An extraordinarily significant contribution that occupied much of his time during the late 1950's and 1960's was his role as co-editor, with D. N. Freedman, of the Doubleday Anchor Bible series. This series provided new translations of the books of the Bible by the best scholars available in the Jewish, Roman Catholic, and Protestant communities, and emphasized literary rather than theological aspects, while incorporating new cultural evidence stemming from archaeological research. As with all publication projects involving a number of authors, the editorial responsibilities were heavy and time consuming. In addition to the editorial work, Albright collaborated with

Stephen Mann in preparing the volume on *Matthew*, which appeared posthumously.

Albright was accorded a great number of honors during his lifetime. He received a host of honorary degrees beginning in 1922 with an Litt.D. from his alma mater,   Upper Iowa University, and from many other American and foreign universities, including:

1936	D.H.L.	Jewish Institute of Religion
1936	D.H.L.	Jewish Theological Seminary
1936	Th.D.	Utrecht University
1946	D.hon.caus.	University of Oslo
1947	LL.D.	Boston College
1948	D.H.L.	Hebrew Union College
1949	LL.D.	St. Andrews University, Scotland
1950	D.H.L.	College of Jewish Studies, Chicago
1951	Litt.D.	Yale University
1952	Litt.D.	Georgetown University
1952	Th.D.	University of Uppsala
1953	Litt.D.	Trinity College, University of Dublin
1954	LL.D.	Franklin and Marshall College
1956	D.Phil.	Hebrew University, Jerusalem
1956	D.C.L.	Pace College
1958	Pd.D.	La Salle College
1960	Litt.D.	Loyola College, Baltimore
1960	Litt.D.	Loyola University, Chicago
1961	L.H.D.	Manhattan College
1961	H.H.D.	Wayne State University
1962	Litt.D.	Harvard University
1962	H.H.D.	Brigham Young University
1964	LL.D.	The Johns Hopkins University
1966	Litt.D.	Lake Erie College
1966	L.H.D.	Colby College
1967	L.H.D.	Dropsie College
1969	L.H.D.	Yeshiva University

He was also named an honorary or corresponding member of many distinguished learned societies and academies of other countries, including:

British Academy
Royal Flemish Academy
Royal Danish Academy
Acádemie des Inscriptions et Belles Lettres, Institut de France
Royal Irish Academy
Austrian Academy of Sciences

Archaeological Survey of India
Royal Asiatic Society
Société Asiatique
British Society for Old Testament Study
Glasgow Oriental Society
German Archaeological Institute

He served as President of the Palestine Oriental Society (1921-22, 1934-35), First Vice-President of the American Schools of Oriental Research for 33 years, President of the American Oriental Society (1935-36), President of the Society of Biblical Literature (1939), Vice-President of the Linguistic Society of America (1941), Vice-President of the Archaeological Institute of America (1949), Vice-Chairman (1939) and member of the American Council of Learned Societies, Vice-President (1956-59) and member of the American Philosophical Society, President of the International Organization of Old Testament Scholars (1956-59), and he was elected to membership in the National Academy of Sciences in 1955. Among the notable awards that he received were: A prize of $10,000 for distinguished scholarship in the humanities by the American Council of Learned Societies; the title "Yaqqir Yerushalayim," which was bestowed in 1969 by Mayor Kollek of Jerusalem, making him the first Gentile and non-Jerusalemite to receive the title; the Archaeological Institute of America Gold Medal for Distinguished Archaeological Achievement in 1969; the Mark Lidzbarski Gold Medal for Excellence in Semitic Studies by the International Congress of Orientalists in 1971. The American Schools of Oriental Research accorded Albright two honors in 1970, dedicating the 200th number of the *Bulletin of the American Schools of Oriental Research* to him in celebration of his service as Editor of the journal for 38 years, and renaming the American School in Jerusalem, with which he had been associated for so long, the W. F. Albright Institute of Archaeological Research.

For his 80th birthday in May, 1971, Albright was honored at a reception in Evergreen House in Baltimore by many former students and friends, and another *Festschrift*, edited by Hans Goedicke of the Department of Near Eastern Studies, the Johns Hopkins University, was presented to him, entitled *Near Eastern Studies in Honor of William Foxwell Albright*. Less than two months later, on July 9, 1971, Albright suffered a stroke that left him semi-conscious until his death on September 19, 1971.

Albright left a scholarly legacy of more than 1000 publications, including books, articles, and reviews. The vast majority contain solutions to problems, new insights, interpretations, and syntheses that have lasting value and must be considered in future research; this will be abundantly clear in the symposium papers that follow.

But Albright also left a legacy of students who have become respected scholars and teachers in diverse disciplines and institutions. The group is large; while an exact count is not known, his students certainly number between 75 and 100, including 57 who received their Ph.D. degrees, seven or eight who began their programs under Albright but completed their degrees after his retirement, and a number who spent one or more years in advanced study but did not take degrees. A common training provided a strong tie that binds all of his pupils together. That training stressed a holistic approach to the cultural history of the ancient Near East.

In view of the fact that this publication is entirely by his students, it is useful to describe the salient features of the Oriental Seminary program. Albright, full-time professor, lectured in history and archaeology, taught Akkadian, Egyptian, Ugaritic, Ethiopic, advanced Hebrew, and conducted seminars in the biblical text; part-time professors Frank R. Blake and Samuel Rosenblatt taught comparative Semitic grammar and Hebrew grammar, and Arabic and Judaica respectively. The most notable feature of the program was a core curriculum, consisting of four, three-year courses in the following subjects, with one year devoted to each of the areas listed in the parentheses: (1) Hebrew Grammar (phonology, morphology, and syntax); (2) Comparative Semitic Grammar (phonology, morphology, and syntax); (3) Ancient Near Eastern History (prehistory, third-second millennia B.C., and first millennium B.C.); and (4) the Archaeology of the Ancient Near East (Egypt, Mesopotamia, Levant). Everyone read Hebrew Bible at whatever level of competence, progressing from beginner to proficient that enabled participation in advanced seminars in various biblical books utilizing, of course, different recensions and different ancient languages. Most students also took at least one and normally several reading courses in Akkadian, Ugaritic, Arabic, Aramaic and Syriac; fewer studied Egyptian, Ethiopic, Sumerian, and Hittite. This core curriculum was required of all students with very few exceptions. Specialization was primarily manifest in dissertation topics and by taking additional courses in the Oriental Seminary or in other departments of the university. Most of the students were primarily interested in biblical scholarship, and therefore took more courses in ancient Near Eastern languages and literatures. An archaeologist also enrolled in courses in Greek and Roman archaeology given by the Classics Department, while a linguist took courses in Sanskrit, Old Norse, Greek, Latin, etc. in the various departments.

Oriental Seminary classes had no semester or year-end examinations; ultimately written examinations were given upon completion of class work, the timing of which was decided by Albright. These examinations covered all subjects studied whether one had been in attendance three years or ten. They were given on the honor system but with no ponies or "open books" permitted. Normally each examination required from eight to twenty-four hours to write, and it was permissible to have a free day or two for rest, changing subject focus, and last-minute review before going on to the next examination.

Dissertation preparation generally followed the examinations, and when completed, it was formally submitted to the university. Then the humanities oral examination was given and if passed, the degree was awarded.

The core curriculum indoctrinated students in all major fields of study, and engendered a respect for the contributions of each field; a philologian understood the importance of archaeology, and an archaeologist understood the basic structure and relationships of the languages. Thus, students were forced to be generalists before becoming specialists. While such an orientation to Near Eastern studies seems obviously desirable, surprisingly few other graduate schools fostered it.

With the growth of the Oriental Seminary and the increasing influence of its graduates in major institutions of learning, Albright referred to his pupils and their shared point of view as the "Baltimore School," a name he preferred to the "Albright School," which was sometimes used by other scholars. It was a "school" not only in the sense of a master teacher and his pupils, but also in terms of the breadth of the school's emphasis and curriculum. There is no better measure of this breadth--and of Albright's wide-ranging knowledge---than the diversity of the 57 Ph.D. dissertation topics he supervised. While these may be classified in several different ways, and while the subject boundaries are sometimes blurred, the following categories present the case. It should be noted that philology played a major role in all topics, though less so in archaeological dissertations.

Discipline	Dissertations
Bible	23
History	11
Linguistics	9
Archaeology	5
Akkadian	4
Egyptian	2
Literary (non-biblical)	3

Albright was more than a teacher to many of his students; he was also a friend and something of a father figure, who took a personal interest in their achievements and their tribulations. This role was understood by students, family, and all who were close to him. Upon his death in Baltimore, Maryland, September 19, 1971, Mrs. Albright asked her sons to inform as many former students as possible. Her message not only announced the time and place of the funeral, but also included the hope that "his boys would come." And they came.

The Contributions of W. F. Albright to
Semitic Epigraphy and Palaeography

Frank Moore Cross, Jr.

Harvard University

Albright was a master of the typological sciences. He was expert in the minute details which properly mark typological analysis, master of the meticulous method by which typological features must be arranged in sequences and patterns. He made maximal use of the typological sciences in establishing his ceramic chronology of the land of Israel in the Bronze and Iron ages, indeed, in analyzing artifacts from the common potsherd to grand objects of art and architecture. He arranged signs and scripts, linguistic features and spelling styles, prosodic forms and even religious ideas in evolutionary patterns and sequences of patterns. He was intent on assigning relative dates to typological change, sequence dating, and, when evidence permitted, to establishing absolute dates. In such fashion, he moved from typological analysis, with its analogies to scientific method, to historical synthesis, especially in the field of the history of culture. He hoped to write "scientific history" using the weapons of the typological sciences in a war against idealistic practitioners of historiography. Indeed, his chief contribution to historical method, or the philosophy of historical method, can be discovered in his instincts and habits developed as a typologist.

I think it is fair to say that Albright never fully articulated his philosophy of historical method. His Aristotelian stance in metaphysics and theology did not permit him to state his position with clarity. In fact, in historical method he sided with the logical positivists and analytical philosophers.

My assigned task is to evaluate Albright's contributions to epigraphy and palaeography. Here his skills as a typologist are most in evidence. I must admit that epigraphy and palaeography are not inspiring topics to address in general terms. Their excitement is found in the shape of a letter, or in a missing vowel letter, in short in microscopic detail. I am reminded of A. E. Houseman's observation. He stated that no headier feeling can be experienced by a humanist than that which comes when an original reading of a text, won by his brilliant emendation, is subsequently confirmed in a newly found manuscript. The thrills of palaeographic, of epigraphic discovery belong often to the same order of esoteric scholarship.

Some definitions are in order. Epigraphy and palaeography are used here (and generally in our field) in a narrowed sense. By "epigraphy" we

17

mean the study and interpretation of inscriptions on hard surfaces, stone, metal, pottery, and so on, and especially, in the present context, Semitic inscriptions in alphabetic scripts. "Palaeography," properly a broad term applied to the study of ancient written documents, we shall restrict to the study of ancient scripts, their decipherment, the description of their origin and development, and above all their dating by typological analysis.

There is a tendency among scholars today to denigrate Albright as a scholar by observing that he was not a specialist--in archaeology, history or biblical studies. He was an Orientalist, a generalist, who chose the whole of the Near East as his bailiwick--its archaeology and geography, its languages and literature, its history and religions. Had he not been a generalist, I doubt that we would be gathered here to do him homage. At the same time, it should be said that Albright was a generalist with a specialist's precision and intricate learning in designated fields of oriental inquiry. Albright was in fact an expert, a specialist in West Semitic epigraphy and palaeography. While the number of his papers was relatively few in these fields compared with his publications on archaeological and historical topics, his epigraphic and palaeographical studies gave order and methodological discipline to the field. All of us build on the solid foundations he laid. As his scholarly offspring, we are obliged to honor him.

In 1937, Albright published a paper entitled "A Biblical Fragment from the Maccabaean Age: the Nash Papyrus" (1937:145-176). He undertook to date this unique papyrus containing the Decalogue and the Shemaʻ. He dated the Papyrus, commonly assigned to the early centuries of the Christian era, to the second half of the second century B.C., or more broadly to the Maccabaean Age: 165-37 B.C. Today, with dated documents of the Persian, Hellenistic, and Roman periods, as well as hundreds of relatively dated documents from the Jordan rift, including some 600 Qumran scrolls, we should date the Nash Papyrus to about 175 to 150 B.C. In my paper, "The Development of the Jewish Scripts" (1961:133-202, esp. 148), I dated the Nash Papyrus to 150 B.C. Avigad, after reviewing the Qumran manuscripts in 1957, dated the Papyrus to the second half of the second century, precisely Albright's date.

More important than the dating of the Papyrus itself, was Albright's tracing of the development of the Aramaic scripts from the seventh century to the end of the Persian period, and the emergence of national scripts in the Hellenistic age. He argued that they descended from the Aramaic hands of the late Persian chancelleries: the Nabataean script, the Palmyrene script, the Jewish National script, and finally, the emergence of the Herodian book hand (the so-called square character) in the Roman period. In this extraordinary paper, he organized the field of late Aramaic and Jewish palaeography once and for all. He marked out the main lines of evolution of the scripts. He noted the pitfalls of dating one national script by another national script, after their divergence from the ancestral Aramaic character. In short, Albright laid down the principles of sound palaeographical method in the course of dating a particular Jewish hand.

In the early spring of 1948, some photographs of the great Isaiah Scroll (1QIsa$_a$) were sent to Albright from the American School in Jerusalem. Albright immediately dated this scroll to the second century B.C., roughly contemporary with the Nash Papyrus, and cabled Jerusalem congratulating them on "the greatest discovery of modern times." John Trever, a fellow of the American School, who must also be credited with recognizing the antiquity of the Dead Sea Scrolls that were brought to the school in Jerusalem, based his judgment on Albright's analysis of the Nash Papyrus. The antiquity of the manuscripts of Qumrân, Cave 1 was earlier recognized by Professor E. L. Sukenik. Sukenik, who had spent a year as a student of Albright at the American School in Jerusalem, knew well Albright's paper on the Nash Papyrus and was himself an authority on the ossuary inscriptions of the Herodian Age. Noel Freedman and I remember the events of these days well. We were working--reading--in our carrels in the Johns Hopkins library when Albright rushed in and fetched us to his study. He showed us Trever's photographs of the Isaiah Scroll and commented in detail on their palaeographical features. Neither of us disputed his analysis. We did somehow seduce Albright into giving us the photographs for overnight study, and the night was spent in working on the script and the text of the Isaiah scroll.

The battle of the dating of the scrolls then began. In 1949, Albright wrote a brief paper (1949:10-19) summarizing new data which had come to light since his Nash paper, that is, in the interval between 1937 and the discoveries at Qumrân a decade later. As a matter of fact, Albright had carefully collected the new evidence in preparation for a new study bringing his Nash paper up to date when word of the scroll discoveries came from Jerusalem. Most trained palaeographers and epigraphists, whose expertise predated the discovery of the Qumrân scrolls and the controversy over their date, argued for a pre-70 date for the manuscripts and many agreed with Albright's date in the second century B.C. for the large Isaiah scroll (1QIsa$_a$). Among them were Birnbaum in England, Rosenthal and Ginsberg in America, Sukenik, Avigad, and de Vaux in Jerusalem. A notable exception was a most respected scholar, an experienced epigraphist and the dominant Semitist in England, G. R. Driver, later Lord Driver. In a monograph on the scrolls, Driver (1951:23-48) remarks that the date of the scrolls is "an exceedingly difficult question to answer." Then in a scornful footnote, he remarks that "Professor Albright answered this question in one hour...!" Driver, after proper study and reflection, several years in fact, dated the scrolls to the era "between the Mishnah and the Talmud, somewhere between A.D. 200 and A.D. 500. A date toward the end rather than the beginning of this period is indicated..." Driver was wrong on two counts. His dating was roughly a half millennium in error. Furthermore, Albright dated the Isaiah scroll in five minutes, not in an hour. He merely waited an hour before announcing the date, checking and rechecking this sensational evidence. Or to be more precise, Albright was uniquely prepared by a decade and more of research in Jewish palaeography to fix the date of the Isaiah scroll. In all events, now after some 35 years, we can state categorically, that his dates were accurate within 50 years, and that his paper on the Nash Papyrus is the keystone of all subsequent work in the field of Jewish palaeography.

Albright's contribution to the study of old Hebrew inscriptions was not slight. In his first paper on epigraphy in 1926 (1926:75-102), he attempted to decipher the ostracon found in the City of David, the so-called Ophel ostracon of the late seventh or early sixth century B.C. His drawing of the ostracon and its script was accurately done, and is still useful. It may be worth noting in passing that Albright did all of his drawings of inscriptions and scripts, and, so far as I am aware, every major palaeographer does his own drawings. On the one hand, the palaeographer trusts no one else to draw the forms of letters accurately in size, stance, and shading. On the other hand, it is in the process of repeatedly tracing letters that he learns typological detail which permits him to decipher and date texts.

In 1932, Albright (1932:77-106) wrote a long and brilliant paper on the Seal of Eliakim, the steward of Yawkin. The Seal, preserved in sealings from Tell Beit Mirsim, Ramat Raḥel, and Beth-shemesh, was identified by Albright as belonging to the steward of Jehoiachin, King of Judah, who went into exile in 597.

Albright argued further that Eliakim was steward of the crown properties in the years 597-587 while Jehoiachin was in exile, that is during the regency of Zedekiah. The Seal became a linchpin, so to speak, for the chronology of Judah, dating the fall of Tell Beit Mirsim and Beth-shemesh to 587. Furthermore, it became the centerpiece in an argument concerning the date of Lachish Stratum III. The Eliakim Seals were associated with the Royal Stamped Jar Handles in Tell Beit Mirsim, and at Lachish; at the latter, these handles were found in sealed deposits of Stratum III. The archaeological community was divided sharply. One group, including Albright, Kathleen Kenyon, and G. Ernest Wright, dated the fall of Lachish, city III, to Nebuchadnezzar in 597; another group, following Olga Tufnell, dated the fall of city III to Sennacherib in 701 B.C. The issue was not merely a matter of dating Lachish III, but also of dating administrative innovations represented by the Royal Jar Handles (either to Hezekiah or Josiah), and above all the corpus of pottery types that marked either the late eighth or early sixth century in Israel, according to the solution of the problem.

Unhappily, Albright was wrong in his dating of the Eliakim sealings. In 1973 I argued on linguistic and palaeographical grounds that the seal could be no later than the eighth century (Cross 1983:58). In papers on new excavations at Lachish, David Ussishkin (1976:1-13; 1977:28-60; 1978:76-81; 1983: 160-164) demonstrated beyond cavil that both the Eliakim sealings and the Royal Handles were late eighth century in date on archaeological grounds, and that Lachish III fell to Sennacherib. It should be said that Albright's error in dating the Seal (he was roughly a century off) was a small one given the comparative data available in 1932. Nevertheless, the error introduced confusion into the archaeological chronology for the end of Judah for 40 years.

The discovery of the main group of Lachish Ostraca in 1935 and their *editio princeps* in 1938 stimulated Albright to write a series of papers (1938:11-17), (1939:16-21), and (1941:18-24) dealing with these important texts written in the Hebrew of the era of Jeremiah. His translations, by and large the best available today, appear in *Ancient Near Eastern Texts* (1950:321-322). Albright's contribution to the decipherment and interpretation of the letters was major, rivaled only by H. L. Ginsberg's work, I think. He contributed a number of sound readings and solutions to points of difficulty; equally or more important, he recognized the good readings of other scholars, separating wheat from chaff, and repudiated more adventuresome and sensational readings, especially those of Torczyner (Tur-Sinai). The study of these letters has progressed little since Albright's day, despite a burgeoning bibliography. The most significant advances in decipherment have been made by André Lemaire (1977:87-143) whose keen eye for form has solved a number of obscure readings. Yigael Yadin's recent audacious proposals (1985:141-145) are brilliant, but in my judgment, wrong.

Albright was occupied throughout his lifetime with the study of inscriptions written in Early Linear Phoenician. In 1925, he spent three days studying the archaic Phoenician inscription engraved on the magnificent sarcophagus of 'Aḥirâm, king of Byblus. The sarcophagus, found in 1923 and published by René Dussaud in 1924 had created a scholarly sensation. In the tomb shaft were found fragments of alabaster vases bearing the cartouche of Ramesses II, and it was confidently assumed that the inscription and its archaic script dated to the 13th century B.C. Albright's first paper on the 'Aḥirâm text from Byblus appeared in 1926 (1926:122-127). Even in this first paper, Albright shows lack of ease with the 13th century date. Aware that the 10th century inscriptions from Byblus, the Eliba'l inscription on a statue of Osorkon I, and the Abiba'l inscription on the statue of Shishak, were written in a script little evolved beyond the hand of the 'Aḥirâm scribe, in a paper written in 1942, he lowered his date for 'Aḥirâm to ca. 1000 B.C., partly on archaeological and partly on palaeographical grounds, making 'Aḥirâm of Byblus a contemporary of David and of 'Aḥirâm--biblical Hiram--of Tyre. In 1943, Aimé-Giron (1943:284ff.) independently dated the 'Aḥirâm text to the 10th century. However, most scholars held firm for the earlier date, including Maurice Dunand, who published his *Byblia Grammata* with its rich content of new material from Byblus in 1945. Dunand argued strongly for the 13th century date, and indeed for a 16th or 17th century date for the Shipiṭ-ba'l inscription, which he published in the volume. In 1946, Binyamin Mazar (1946:166-181; later, 1986:231-247) argued for dating the 'Aḥirâm inscriptions to the 10th century, and in the same year Dunand, in a post-scriptum to his book, *Byblia Grammata*, circulated after the book was published, reduced the date of 'Aḥirâm to about 1000 on the basis of Iron I pottery found in some unexcavated debris in the shaft of the 'Aḥirâm tomb. Albright's definitive treatment of the Byblian inscriptions of the l0th century appeared in the *Journal of the American Oriental Society* (1947:153-160). While one occasionally finds a 13th century date for 'Aḥirâm in handbooks on the alphabet, both Albright's dating and his ordering of the Byblian inscriptions have been accepted by the younger generations of epigraphists. Once again, Albright brought chronological order and typological discipline to a field in chaos: in this case, the evolution of Earlier Linear Phoenician scripts.

Two other major papers in this field should be mentioned: the study of the Gezer Calendar in 1943 (Albright 1943:16-26), and a study entitled "New Light on the Early History of Phoenician Colonization" (Albright 1942:14-22). In the latter paper, Albright discussed the Archaic Cyprus inscription, advancing its decipherment, and dating it firmly to the ninth century, preferring the first half of the century, and more important, the group of three Archaic Phoenician inscriptions from Sardinia, all three of which he dated to the ninth century. There is now consensus among palaeographers that the Nora Stone is late ninth century and the Bosa Fragment no later than the ninth. The Nora fragment, a small portion of a stele of monumental size, is clearly earlier, and best fits into a group of llth century inscriptions found in the 40 years after Albright's paper was written. I have written on the Fragment in three papers: The first in 1974, the most recent to be published in the Lambdin volume, based on a reexamination of the Stone in September of 1984 (1974:490-493; 1979:97-123; 1986:16-130).

On the basis of these texts, Albright argued anew for the early expansion of the Phoenicians into the central and western Mediterranean. His views ran counter to the consensus in the field, that Phoenician maritime activity and early colonization did not begin before the eighth or even the seventh century B.C. Opposition to his views still runs strong. However, hard evidence is slowly accumulating in his support. From Cyprus has come a 12th century text in reduced Canaanite cuneiform, and the excavations at Kition by Karageorghis have uncovered a Phoenician temple founded no later than the mid-tenth century, and perhaps in the llth. At Tekke in Crete, a bronze bowl has been uncovered that I have dated to the end of the llth century B.C. (1980:1-20, and references, notably M. Sznycer, "L'Inscription phénicienne de Tekke près de Cnossus," *Kadmos* 18:89-93). Lipinski has recently scolded me for dating it too early, and then with delicate precision dates it to 1000 B.C. Presumably, my date was a year early. Emile Puech has followed my early dating (1983:365-395). From Spain has comes a text dedicated to Hurrian Astarte dated to the eighth century, probably the third-quarter of the eighth century (Cross 1971:189-195; cf. Puech 1977:85-92). Solá-solé dates it to the first half of the eighth century. Two Phoenician bronzes of the llth century have recently been found in Nuraghic centers in Sardinia (Barreca 1971:7-27; 1980:475-486; 1986:131-143; cf. Bisi 1977:910-932; Tore 1981:11-25).

I believe it is now clear that Phoenician sailors and metallurgists were on the seas of the central and western Mediterranean, perhaps as early as the late 12th century, certainly in the 11th century, reopening trade routes plied by their Canaanite forebears, notably the ships of Ugarit before the cataclysm that brought to an end the Late Bronze Age in 1200 B.C. I do not believe that systematic attempts at colonization in the west need be dated before the late ninth century when it is documented in Sardinia. In the interim, we suspect that traders and metallurgists were left behind in western ports from time to time to live happily and profitably with the native populace, and perhaps to set up refineries (hence with Albright, the term *tarshish*). I should add that new evidence has accumulated pointing to an 11th century date for the borrowing of the Phoenician alphabet, probably in the vicinity of Crete where the most archaic Greek scripts (from a typological point of view) have been found (Cross 1986:124). This supports Albright's case as well, though he himself argued for a borrowing no earlier than the ninth century B.C.

Albright's treatment of the Gezer Calendar is a classic. He argued for a 10th century date for the Calendar, and his dating is now generally accepted. More important, I believe, is his analysis of the orthography of the inscription. Albright recognized that it was written in the style of the Phoenician chancelleries, that is, with no vowel letters either in medial or in final positions. He never set out in systematic form his understanding of the development of Hebrew orthographic styles. One finds isolated observations in the paper on the Gezer Calendar, and in his treatment of the Balaam Oracles (1944:207-233). It is evident, however, that he had perceived a sequence of orthographic styles, and recognized their importance, both for their chronological significance, and as a control in deciphering difficult or obscure texts.

We have been following a reverse chronology in our review of Albright's epigraphic labors, beginning with late Jewish and Aramaic scripts, and moving backward to Hebrew and then to early Phoenician epigraphy. This brings us finally to Albright's work on old Canaanite inscriptions and alphabetic origins. Albright's first major paper on old Canaanite was entitled, "Some Suggestions for the Decipherment of the Proto-Sinaitic Inscriptions," (1935:334-340). It is published in the same issue of the *Journal of the Palestine Oriental Society* with his Presidential Address. The *Journal*, it may be noted, was edited in 1935 by Albright and Danby, with Abel and Alt as editorial advisors, and credits a young student, G. Ernest Wright, with editorial assistance. The 30's were extraordinary times in Jerusalem with such scholars as Alt, Albright, Vincent, Abel, and Mayer, and the youngsters Ginsberg, Mazar, and de Vaux exchanging views and reading papers.

Albright's first paper on the inscriptions from Sinai was noteworthy, primarily for its insistence that any decipherment of these early texts must reckon with additional Canaanite phonemes beyond the twenty-two of Linear

Phoenician: ḥ and ḫ, '(ʾayin) and ǵ(ġayin), t and š, and that Egyptian and cuneiform sources for Canaanite in the second millennium must be scrutinized if the successful decipherment were to be achieved. His actual essay in decipherment made little progress. He returned to the Sinaitic texts in the paper published in *BASOR* (1948:6-22). In this paper, occasioned by a visit to Serâbît el-Khâdem and to Cairo, where he collated texts, he made major advances toward decipherment. Particularly important was his recognition that the texts were 15th century B.C. (1500 in round numbers), not 18th century as generally supposed. Some 19 out of some 27 original signs were correctly identified. I think it is fair to say that this paper made the first real advance in the decipherment of these difficult texts since Sir Alan Gardiner's stunning paper published in 1916 (1916:1-16).

Albright returned to the Proto-Sinaitic texts finally in 1966, publishing his monograph, *The Proto-Sinaitic Inscriptions and Their Decipherment*, interestingly enough, in the *Harvard Theological Studies*. Further advances toward decipherment were made in this monograph. New discoveries of old Canaanite texts were integrated into his description of the evolution of the early alphabet. Yet Albright was aware that his decipherment was not complete or definitive. New texts were needed. Six or seven graphemes were not yet identified. Excessively imaginative reconstructions of obscure readings mar Albright's final essay. New discoveries have filled in some gaps in our knowledge of old Canaanite alphabetic signs. Abecedaries in Ugaritic have made certain Albright's claims that Canaanite north and south in the Late Bronze age possessed additional phonemes and hence additional signs.

Albright's assumption, too, that both the order and names of the alphabetic signs go back to the invention of the alphabet is supported by new evidence. He lived to see his vindication in these matters, and rejoiced in print. In the last years, important new material in Proto-Canaanite from Phoenicia and Israel has been found: the ʿIzbet Ṣarṭa sherd with an abecedary of the early 12th century, the Qubur Walaydah sherd of ca. 1200, a newly published ostracon from Lachish inscribed in boustrophedon style from the 13th century (Cross 1984:71-76), and a score of inscribed arrowheads of the late 12th and 11th centuries (Cross:1980:1-20). Each new discovery has given support to the general lines of Albright's decipherment. I have little doubt that some surprises are still in store for us. Byforms of signs are appearing in the new texts. We now know the original pictograph for *zayin*. The evolution of the alphabet is more complex than any of us had anticipated. Of course at any stage of knowledge, one must propose the most parsimonious solution to explain extant data. But history, including the history of the alphabet, does not always obey Occam's rule. In any case, Albright's lifelong assumption that the alphabet was invented by the Canaanites under the inspiration of Egyptian hieroglyphic writing, and based on a principle of acrophony is established.

With the first publication of the Ugaritic texts, Albright addressed himself energetically to problems of decipherment, grammatical analysis, interpretation and translation of these difficult 14th century texts. In a series of essays (1932b:15-20; 1932c:185-208; 1933:13-20; 1934:101,140), he tackled the most important of the texts. Throughout his scholarly life he returned again and again to deal with specific difficult passages. Albright brought to Ugaritic studies perhaps a unique knowledge of Canaanite and related dialects of the late second millennium.

By 1929, he had solved the mysteries of Egyptian syllabic orthography, a system used by Egyptian scribes to vocalize foreign words and names. His major monograph on Egyptian syllabic orthography was published in 1934 (Albright 1934), and met with rigid rejection by most Egyptologists. Over the decades, however, it has steadily gained acceptance by younger Egyptologists. In solving the problems of Egyptian syllabic orthography, Albright perceived order and typological development in orthographic practice considered chaotic and purely arbitrary, with each scribe going his own way without orthographic convention restraining him. We have noted Albright's contribution to the history of Phoenician and Hebrew orthographic principles. Perhaps I should add that late Punic and Neo-Punic writing, still treated by virtually all scholars as having no spelling rules or convention, has begun to yield to orthographic analysis.

In addition to his knowledge of Canaanite embedded in Egyptian transcriptions, Albright also was an assiduous student of the Canaanite substratum of the Amarna Letters. In 1937, he published his elegant study of the Egyptian correspondence of Abi-milki (1937b:190-203). His magisterial edition of the Jerusalem Letters was never published for reasons I do not know. Many of his insights are to be found, however, in his translations in *Ancient Near Eastern Texts* (with George E. Mendenhall). Perhaps the most important monograph written on the grammar of Amarna Canaanite is to be found in the unpublished dissertation on the Byblian Letters, by his student, William Moran (1950).

To return to Albright's contribution to Ugaritic studies, we find Albright approaching these texts, written in what he calls "North Canaanite," with an unrivaled grasp of Canaanite materials and Egyptian and Akkadian sources.

He participated in the solution of the last, thorniest problems of the decipherment of the script, the proper analysis of the signs representing ẓ (emphatic ṯ in Proto-Semitic reconstruction), and worked out a solution as to the phonetic development of the sibilants. He was the first to describe fully the system of case-endings used in Ugaritic, and maintained from the beginning the essentially Canaanite character of the verbal system. Friedrich described the modal endings of the verb, and Ginsberg the operation of Barth's law in verbal forms.

It is difficult to assess an individual scholar's contribution to the translation of the Ugaritic texts, their grammatical and lexical analysis, and the ultimate exegesis of the Ugaritic mythic cycles and epics. Many scholars made distinguished contributions. I have no doubt that Albright was a major figure in early Ugaritic research. In honesty, however, I believe that the giant in the early field was H. L. Ginsberg. Perhaps more than any other scholar, he correctly perceived the grammatical structure of Ugaritic and sketched the base of subsequent Ugaritic grammar. His translations were unrivaled when first set out, and his sections in *Ancient Near Eastern Texts* (Ginsberg 1950:129-155) are classics, more influential in the history of the field than any others, still to be consulted by any serious student. Even the style of his English translations set a standard for excellence.

To sum up, W. F. Albright distinguished himself in most of the major fields of West Semitic epigraphy: in Jewish and late Aramaic palaeography, in Hebrew and early Phoenician epigraphy, in the decipherment of Old Canaanite, in solving the system of Egyptian syllabic orthography, in Amarna studies, in Ugaritic research. While he was not *facile princeps* in all of these fields, to use one of his favorite Ciceronian expressions, when we survey the epigraphic and palaeological fields as a whole, he proves to be the giant of giants in his generation of scholars.

References

Aimé-Giron, N.
   1943   *Annales du Service des Antiquités de l´Ägypte* 42:284ff. [*apud* B. Mazar].

Albright, W. F.
   1926   "Notes on Early Hebrew and Aramaic Epigraphy," *Journal of the Palestine Oriental Society* 6:75-102.

   1927   "The End of the Inscription on the Ahiram Sarcophagus," *Journal of the Palestine Oriental Society* 7:122-127.

   1932a   "The Seal of Eliakim and the Latest Preexilic History of Judah, with some Observations on Ezekiel," *Journal of Biblical Literature* 51:77-106.

   1932b   "New Light on Early Canaanite Language and Literature," *Bulletin of the American Schools of Oriental Research* 45:15-20.

   1932c   "The North-Canaanite Epic of 'Al'êyân Ba'al and Môt," *Journal of the Palestine Oriental Society* 12:185-208.

   1933   "More Light on the Canaanite Epic of 'Al'êyân Ba'al and Môt," *Bulletin of the American Schools of Oriental Research* 50:13-20.

   1934   "The North-Canaanite Poems of 'Al'êyân Ba'ai and the 'Gracious Gods'," *Journal of the Palestine Oriental Society* 14:101-140.

   1934   *The Vocalization of the Egyptian Syllabic Orthography.* American Oriental Series 5. New Haven.

   1935   "Some Suggestions for the Decipherment of the Proto-Sinaitic Inscriptions," *Journal of the Palestine Oriental Society* 15:334-340.

   1937a   "A Biblical Fragment from the Maccabaean Age: the Nash Papyrus," *Journal of Biblical Literature* 56:145-176.

   1937b   "The Egyptian Correspondence of Abi-milki, Prince of Tyre," *Journal of Egyptian Archaeology* 23:190-203.

1938   "The Oldest Hebrew Letters: the Lachish Ostraca," *Bulletin of the American Schools of Oriental Research* 70:11-17.

1939   "A Reexamination of the Lachish Letters," *Bulletin of the American Schools of Oriental Research* 73:16-21.

1941   "The Lachish Letters after Five Years," *Bulletin of the American Schools of Oriental Research* 82:18-24.

1942   "New Light on the Early History of Phoenician Colonization," *Bulletin of the American Schools of Oriental Research* 83:14-22.

1943   "The Gezer Calendar," *Bulletin of the American Schools of Oriental Research* 92:16-26.

1944   "The Oracles of Balaam," Journal of Biblical Literature 63:207-233.

1947   "The Phoenician Inscriptions of the Tenth Century B.C. from Byblus," *Journal of the American Oriental Society* 67:153-160.

1948   "The Early Alphabetic Inscriptions from Sinai and Their Decipherment," *Bulletin of the American Schools of Oriental Research* 110:6-22.

1949   "On the Date of the Scrolls from Ain Feshkha and the Nash Papyrus," *Bulletin of the American Schools of Oriental Research* 115:10-19.

1950   "The Lachish Ostraca," in J. B. Pritchard, editor, *Ancient Near Eastern Texts*. Princeton:Princeton University Press.

Avigad, N.
1957   *The Palaeography of the Dead Sea Scrolls and Related Documents*. Offprint from *Aspects of the Dead Sea Scrolls, Scripta Hierosolymitana* IV. Jerusalem:Hebrew University.

Barreca, F.
1971   "Sardegna," *L´Espansione fenicia nel Mediterraneo. Studi Semitici* 38. Rome:Consiglio Nazionale della Ricerche. Pp. 7-27.

1980   "Contatti tra protosardi e fenici," *Atti della XXII riunione scientifica dell´ Istituto Italiano di Preistoria e Protostoria*. Florence. Pp. 475-486.

1986   "Phoenicians in Sardinia: The Bronze Figurines," in M. Balmuth, editor, *Studies in Sardinian Archaeology* II. Ann Arbor:University of Michigan Press. Pp. 131-143.

Bisi, A. M.
1977   "L´Apport phénicien aux bronzes nouragigue di Sardaigne," *Latomus* 36:910-932.

Cross, F. M.
1961   "The Development of the Jewish Scripts," in G. Ernest Wright, editor, *The Bible and the Ancient Near East*. Garden City, NY:Doubleday. Pp. 133-202.

1971   "The Old Phoenician inscription from Spain Dedicated to Hurrian Astarte," *Harvard Theological Review* 65:189-195.

1974   "Leaves from an Epigraphist's Notebook: The Oldest Phoenician Inscription from the Western Mediterranean," *Catholic Biblical Quarterly* 36:490-493.

1979   "Early Alphabetic Scripts," in F. M. Cross, editor, *Symposia Celebrating the Seventh-fifth Anniversary of the Founding of the American Schools of Oriental Research*. Cambridge:American Schools of Oriental Research. Pp. 97-123.

1980   "Newly Found Inscriptions in Old Canaanite and Early Phoenician Scripts," *Bulletin of the American Schools of Oriental Research* 238:1-20 and references, notably M. Sznycer, "L´Inscription phénicienne de Tekke près di Cnossus," *Kadmos* 18:89-93.

1983   "The Seal of Miqnêyaw, Servant of Yahweh," in L. Gorelick and E. Williams-Forte, eds., *Ancient Seals and the Bible*. Malibu, CA:Undena. Pp. 55-63.

1984   "An Old Canaanite Inscription Recently Found at Lachish," *Tel Aviv* 11:71-76.

1986   "Phoenicians in the West: The Early Epigraphic Evidence," in M. Balmuth, editor, *Studies in Sardinian Archaeology* II. Ann Arbor:University of Michigan Press. Pp. 116-130.

Driver, G. R.
1951   *The Hebrew Scrolls*. London:Geoffrey Cumberlege; Oxford University Press.

Dunand, M.
1945 *Byblia Grammata*. Beyrouth:Direction des Antiquités.

Gardiner, A.
1916 "The Egyptian Origin of the Semitic Alphabet," *Journal of Egyptian Archaeology* 3:1-16.

Ginsberg, H. L.
1950 "Ugaritic Myths, Epics, and Legends," in J. B. Pritchard, editor, *Ancient Near Eastern Texts*. Princeton:Princeton University Press.

Lemaire, A.
1977 *Inscriptions hébraiques: I Les ostraca*. Paris:Éditions du Cerf.

Lipinski, E.
1983 "Notes d´épigraphie phénicienne et punique," *Orientalia Lovaniensia Periodica* 14:129-165.

Mazar, B.
1986 "The Phoenician Inscriptions from Byblos and the Evolution of the Phoenician-Hebrew Alphabet," in S. Ahituv and B. Levine, editors, *The Early Biblical Period: Historical Essays*. Pp. 231-247. Jerusalem:Israel Exploration Society. This paper originally appeared in *Leshonenu* 14 (1946):166-181.

Moran, W.
1950 "A Syntactical Study of the Dialect of Byblos as Reflected in the Amarna Tablets," unpublished dissertation, Johns Hopkins University.

Puech, E.
1977 "L´Inscription phénicienne du trône d´Astart à Séville," *Revista di Studi Fenici* 5:85-92.

1983 "Présence phénicienne dans les iles a la fin du IIe millenniare," *Revue Biblique* 90:365-395.

Tore, G.
1981 "Bronzetti fenici della Nurra," in *Bronzetti della Nurra*. Quaderni 9. Sassari. Pp. 11-25.

Ussishkin, D.
1976 "Royal Judean Storage Jars and Private Seal Impressions," *Bulletin of the American Schools of Oriental Research* 223:1-13.

1977   "The Destruction of Lachish by Sennacherib and the Dating of the Royal Judean Storage Jars," *Tel Aviv* 4:28-60.

1978   "Excavations at Tel Lachish 1973-1977: Preliminary Report," *Tel Aviv* 5:1-97.

1983   "Excavations at Tel Lachish 1978-1983: Second Preliminary Report," *Tel Aviv* 10:97-181.

Yadin, Y.
    1985   "The Lachish Letters--Originals or Copies and Drafts," *Eretz-Israel* (Avigad Volume):141-145. English translation in Hershel Shanks and B. Mazar, eds., *Recent Archaeology in the Land of Israel*. Washington:Biblical Archaeological Society, 1981. Pp.179-186.

W. F. Albright as an Historian

David Noel Freedman

The University of Michigan

Albright was not an historian: he was interested in history, especially in historical method, concerned to use its resources and techniques in order to achieve results in other areas. If we can speak of him as an historian at all, it will be as an historian of ideas and especially as an historian of religion, not from the point of view of anthropology, but of ideas and their development. What may have been intended in this colloquium to serve as focal point or culmination may prove to be something less than that, since Albright was not one of the great historians of our time. He was neither an encyclopedist such as Eduard Meyer, nor an innovator with fresh ideas, perhaps like Spengler, Sorokin, or even Toynbee, but rather an apologist for a somewhat traditional, even archaic outlook. His model was in truth none of the above, but was rather the great Christian synthesis--acknowledged or not--derived from the major theologians, whether Roman Catholic like Thomas Aquinas or Protestant like John Calvin, between whom there was not such a great difference. There is a debt as well to figures such as Maimonides in Judaism, and no doubt to the Arabic precursors (Avicenna [Ibn-sina] and Averroes [Ibn-rusd]), who created the comprehensive, medieval theological-historical framework on which both Jewish and Christian philosophers were dependent. Behind the medieval synthesis, to which Albright was primarily indebted, lay the last and greatest of the classical syntheses, that of Augustine, who also built on the work of predecessors, but who finally defined the nature and scope of Christian historical apologetics. The *City of God* may be called the true model for Albright's work, although he never really attempted a great synthetic work for our time, but only sketches for such a work--*Prolegomena* as it turned out--much in the mode and mold of the great synthesizer of Old Testament studies, Julius Wellhausen. Even Albright's last great undertaking, *The History of the Religion of Israel*, the title of which clearly defines his interest and objectives, fell far short of a comprehensive much less exhaustive treatment and, even if he had not abandoned it in midcourse, it would never have been the history, or even part of the history, that many looked for. I don't think that Albright ever thought in those terms or that he ever intended to write a definitive history of the ancient Near East; yet he actually contributed much to the history of ideas, or more precisely of religion as a configuration of certain ideas or beliefs, not so much in anthropological or sociological terms as in philosophical or theological terms.

I recall two conversations I had with Albright about such matters, which are really amalgams and distillations of many discussions and remarks he made from time to time. One was about his career as an Assyriologist, and his oft-repeated remark that if his eyesight had been better, he would have continued along the lines indicated by his studies and his dissertation on The Assyrian Deluge Epic. Certainly he was qualified and would have been outstanding, bad eyes or not, but I am dubious. His consuming interest was always the Bible, and had he been officially or technically an Assyriologist, he would have linked it with his studies of the Bible. The fact is that Assyriology was already moving in its own direction and the traditional association was dissolving. It would not have been possible to do what Albright wanted to do and attempted to do, to build the whole ancient Near East around the Bible--hardly the wave of the future, more like the last stand of the traditionalists.

The other point has to do with the history of the ancient Near East. It was thought by some, perhaps many, that Albright would produce the new comprehensive history of the ancient Near East, that he would be the Eduard Meyer of our generation. I remember asking Albright about this matter, and his reply was twofold: 1) that the field was too large for anyone to try to master, and 2) that it would require the combined talents of many scholars to produce such a work. We all know that the new Cambridge Ancient History is just such an effort and doubtless will be the model for the future. But Albright had something else in mind. He used to point out that the best brains and the best trained scholars of the ancient Near East to be found anywhere in those pre-World War I days were all at the University of Berlin, and that Meyer could do his work and consult with the best authorities without leaving his office or at least his building. Thus with the help of the great scholars surrounding him, he could produce a monumental work. Could Albright have done a similar work for our era? Certainly he had the capability and, considering his technical linguistic and archaeological skills, more so than even Meyer. As for colleagues, the Johns Hopkins University was not the University of Berlin, but Albright was not isolated either in the States or in the world; his correspondence was voluminous and extremely important from a purely scholarly point of view. I think the excuses were just that, but they tell us about the man and his real objectives.

At a very early stage in his career it seemed clear that Albright's primary interest was neither in being an Assyriologist nor in being a comprehensive encyclopedic historian. While several of his early major articles reflected his special training and his wide-ranging interests, the twin foci would always remain the Bible on the one hand, and comparative religion--or to be more precise--the religious ideas of the ancient Near East on the other. In all his subsequent major undertakings, he attempted to combine or blend these interests. A brief glance at his books elucidates and confirms this impression:

The Archaeology of Palestine and the Bible, From the Stone Age to Christianity, Archaeology and the Religion of Israel, and *Yahweh and the Gods of Canaan,* are all efforts to place biblical tradition and biblical religion in the context of ancient Near Eastern religion.

We recognize here as well the final choices as to the area, the subject, and the focus. Throughout his career and even in retirement Albright's primary and abiding interest was the Bible, first of all the Hebrew Bible--the Old Testament--and along with it the New Testament. Although he never pretended to be equally at home in the latter as the former, he was certainly no stranger to the New Testament and could justify his work on the New Testament, especially regarding its archaeology and Semitic background. In the same way he could and did defend his excursions into the classical world, both in terms of its archaeology and pottery sequences as well as its epic and literary traditions. Albright's knowledge of Greek and Indo-European was formidable, so we must never make the mistake of supposing that because his interest and his books centered on one topic, he did not range with impressive authority over many related fields. While he had extraordinarily wide interests and, as a good scientist, dealt with often obscure data in their own right and for their own value, he nevertheless saw almost all the materials he worked with as having relational significance, and as belonging to a much larger scheme at the center of which was biblical religion. I almost wrote "revelation" for "religion, "but that would be unfair and inappropriate. While, for those of us who came to the Hopkins fresh from Christian theological seminaries, the presentation and articulation of the data were quite congenial and the Oriental Seminary--the original title of the department, a painfully literal rendering of the German *Orientalische Seminar*--seemed like a continuation of what we had already experienced, namely a strong Christian cultural bias, and an essentially apologetic approach to the subject of religion, especially biblical religion in (or against) its environment, nevertheless, the basis and the method were different.

Albright himself came out of an orthodox, pietistic Methodist background (his parents were self-supporting missionaries in Chile), and all his life he maintained a conservative stance with regard to biblical--by which he meant and we are to understand Christian if not Protestant--religion, and defended this option with considerable force and zeal. But while he was sympathetic with evangelicals and gave more aid and comfort to ultras--i.e., fundamentalists--than perhaps he realized or intended, he himself was careful to present both the Bible and its environment in terms of the history of ideas, and not as a defender of one faith or a particular branch or family of it. Therefore his own brand of faith and religion was not obtrusive or intrusive, although he never made any effort to conceal his position. He never appeared to be personally involved, since the debate and defense were conducted on purely intellectual grounds. Albright believed very much in evolution, as his discussions of the long history of humanity in the ancient Near East show, and his work with archaeological artifacts would always be a prime case in point. He also believed that biblical religion was the outcome of a long history of development of religious ideas and insights. He regarded biblical religion as different from and superior to all other religions of the ancient Near East, and he emphatically asserted the unique character of the Mosaic faith.

He emphasized even more strongly the affinities between biblical religion and its near relatives, especially Canaanite religion, and how different but parallel tendencies and features were already present in the setting in which biblical religion emerged. An interesting point may be made concerning the patriarchs. Albright clearly believed that there was such a group who belonged to the pre-Mosaic age, and did his best to date and place them--- clearly a very conservative position. At the same time, he rejected the biblical depiction of their religion as essentially the same as that of Moses and his successors (i.e., monotheistic in quality if not in formulation), and he reconstructed their religion as not significantly different from that of their neighbors either in Mesopotamia or Canaan, i.e., polytheistic with a dominant triad of deities. Thus he combined the ideas of evolution and mutation, affirming both the difference and originality of biblical religion, especially beginning with Moses, and at the same time its similarities and affinities with the pagan religions from which it emerged.

The presentation has perhaps even more alarming implications because it is not a testimony or proclamation by a believer, but a reasoned argument intended to persuade or convince the hearer or reader. Whatever Albright's personal faith may have been, and I have heard arguments in opposite directions on this point, his public stance, the one affirmed and argued in his writings, is in defense of biblical religion, very close to its classic Christian form. He believed that the case could be made and justified both by the data and by an appeal to reason, and he argued in this fashion in his classic work *From the Stone Age to Christianity*. Monotheism was demonstrably superior to the polytheism from which it sprang, and of the varying forms of biblical or quasi-biblical monotheism (and the *quasi* could be attached to monotheism also), classic Christianity was the most viable intellectually and philosophically. Since he was teaching in a secular university, and had in his classes and seminars students and auditors of many different persuasions and denominations, he was always exceedingly careful not to identify himself with one point of view, but there could be little doubt as to where he stood or the direction in which his arguments moved.

I think it was this quality more than any other that gave his work (at least on the theoretical or philosophical plane) an archaic or old-fashioned tone. It was not so much the arguments themselves, which were couched in modern terms and buttressed by data derived from the most recent discoveries and analyses, as it was the assumption that the intellectual or rational case for this form of religion could be made at all. It was certainly not objective, anthropological or philosophical reporting. So Albright had an evolutionary and an apparently theological model in mind when he presented the case for biblical religion as the survivor and winner of the battles among the competing religions of antiquity. He supported the historical argument with the equally classic apologetic in favor of Greek philosophy and logical reasoning. We may note in passing that while he stressed Greek thought as the necessary adjunct, organizer, and interpreter of biblical religion, he never wrote a sustained treatment--much less a book--on that component of his triad, but see his posthumously published paper, "Neglected Factors in the Greek Intellectual Revolution" (1972:225-242). The great bulk of his writing focussed on the prior and primary element, biblical religion. The union of biblical religion and Greek thought characterized emergent Christianity, which was to win the day against all competitors whether philosophical or religious, or various combinations of both. To this formidable pairing was added the political and socio-economic genius of the Roman empire, thereby creating for perhaps the only time in world history the appropriate concentration of factors making for universality and unity. This obvious and intended goal for humanity was only partially attained in those days, considering how much of the world and its population were outside the Roman empire, and is much more remote in ours.

As I have suggested, the world view and historical interest demonstrated in his major writings are hardly new; they owe their immediate inspiration to the classical Christian syntheses, particularly those of Aquinas and perhaps Calvin (among other Protestants)--and not to the work of historians and other social scientists of our time, although Albright dealt with the latter and interacted with them. Behind the medievals is the towering figure of Augustine, whose *City of God* is the lineal ancestor of *From the Stone Age to Christianity*, Albright's major statement of his own position.

Albright believed that the union of biblical religion and Greek thought had produced and could go on producing a synthesis of doctrine and practice--that is, a philosophical structure with which to understand the world from a theistic point of view, and a guide or manual for living, which represented the fundamental and terminal truth about God, humanity, and the universe. He also believed that the Bible was true, not only in terms of precepts and concepts properly articulated and formulated, but in a historical sense as well. Here is where he parted company with the leading German scholars of his time. He himself was so heavily influenced by his teacher Paul Haupt and by the great Germans of the previous and present generations that the breach over the question of historicity must have caused him great anguish and concern. In the end, he could not accept the prevailing idealism of the German academic or philosophical environment, nor the pervasive scholarly skepticism about confirming or recovering biblical history. The sophisticated solutions offered by von Rad and his associates and followers regarding the problem of the origins of Old Testament religion, and the corresponding ones offered by Bultmann and his followers with respect to the New Testament were basically unacceptable to Albright, who objected more violently to the latter than to the former. Perhaps Albright did not wish to engage or indulge in the epistemological and linguistic debates which have dominated our century. In any case, he opted for an older and simpler resolution: the essential historicity of the biblical narrative going all the way back to patriarchal times.

Since by temperament and acute intelligence he could hardly take sides in the debate between the radicals who challenged the whole historical premise of biblical religion, and the ultra-conservatives who made it an article of faith, thus allowing no possibility of fruitful discussion, Albright tried to find a lever, some external means by which to recover and to restructure an essentially conservative, but also intellectually respectable and scientifically viable position.

Archaeology provided the means, both the clues and the data. For Albright, the category of history was the critical factor in dealing with the Bible. For fundamentalists, history was the expression and outcome of a dogmatic view of scripture; for the radicals, the historical dimension was largely irrecoverable and irrelevant, and in a different way subordinate to that of confession and faith. Neither of the latter groups was particularly interested in finding out what happened, or in showing how the past could be recovered. For the ultra-orthodox, whatever was affirmed must be true, must have happened, simply because it was affirmed. For the radicals, what was important was the affirmation itself, which was true event, regardless of what may actually have happened, or what could be recovered or reconstructed by historical research.

Albright could not forgive either party for obstructing the scientific search for truth: the radicals for surrendering the recovery of the facts in favor of a symbolic and superficial affirmation, a confession without substantive content; the ultra-orthodox for subordinating history to dogma and closing the door to inquiry and verification. He himself was confident that the diligent pursuit of the facts would produce substantial results, by and large vindicating the biblical account and confirming the essential and central traditions of the Bible. In this way the modern discipline of Biblical Archaeology was fashioned, and Ernest Wright became its chief proponent, aided and abetted by a number of Albright students, including Nelson Glueck, John Bright and others.

Archaeology has been carried out in Palestine, i.e., Israel and Jordan, and elsewhere in the Near East for a variety of reasons, but especially the vindication of biblical history. More recently, the discipline has been redefining itself in terms broadly similar to anthropology--to recover and reconstruct societies in their environment. By and large the biblical component has been somewhat diminished, and there is somewhat less talk of the spade in one hand and the Bible in the other, or of proving or disproving biblical statements and stories. The fact is that the combination was somewhat artificial to begin with. There are fundamental differences in direction and method as well as in end products and comparable results; the biblical scholar deals with one kind of material, and the archaeologist with another. On rare but important occasions there is significant contact, and both disciplines gain from the exchange of data and ideas. Often, however, there is no point of contact and nothing significant happens. On the whole, the results have been somewhat disappointing, though perhaps that was to be expected. Palestinian archaeology has had modest success in turning up monumental remains and inscriptional materials, nothing like the quantity discovered in Mesopotamia and Egypt. And while it has been possible to reconstruct the history of those imperial nations in considerable measure from the finds, the same can hardly be said of Israel and Judah. Inscriptions have proved scarce and generally peripheral, though with marked exceptions such as recent finds at Deir 'Allā and Quntillet Ajrud, not to overlook older discoveries such as the ostraca from Samaria and Lachish, and more recent finds at Arad and Beer-sheba. Unwritten materials are extensive to be sure but not always easy to interpret in terms of biblical connections, while confirmations are few and far between.

Albright's great plan and expectation to set the Bible firmly on the foundation of archaeology buttressed by verifiable data of many kinds seem to have foundered, or at least floundered. After all the digging done and being done, how much has been accomplished? The fierce debates and arguments about the relevance of archaeology to the Bible and vice versa indicate that many issues remain unresolved. Still others seem to be caught in suspension: Can anyone say anything with confidence about the patriarchs or the patriarchal age? The fact that skeptical voices now dominate the scene indicates that the Albrightian synthesis has become unglued, and, for example, we are further from a solution to Genesis 14 than we ever were. Archaeology has not proved decisive or even greatly helpful in answering the questions most often asked by biblical scholars, and has failed to prove the historicity of persons and events especially at the early end of the scale.

At the same time, we would be remiss if we dismissed archaeology as another false messiah, which promised much and delivered little. It always and invariably serves as a permanent reminder that in the Bible we are dealing with real people in real places, who lived and worked and played and died and left evidence of their presence. Like it or not, the Bible is about a particular people and events, bound by time and space; it has a historical dimension, which we ignore or bypass at great peril to the message and meaning of this religion. With all the problems engendered by the historical ingredient we cannot avoid it. We do better to grapple with it head on, than to evade it by proclaiming the historicity of the proclamation or of the community making the affirmation, but without reference to the content of the message, which has historical coordinates that demand verification, or at least realistic appraisal. Nor can we seek refuge in dogmatic pronouncement, affirming what needs validation and verification. Without neglecting the literary and canonical aspects of the case, we must affirm the central importance of the historical factor, and insist on facing the question whenever the biblical tradition is under consideration or criticism.

For this insistence we must be permanently grateful to Albright and his creation: biblical archaeology. Nor should we conclude our review of the subject without reference to the many benefits and contributions made to the elucidation and illumination of the Bible by this discipline. Major manuscript discoveries at Qumrân and Ugarit have contributed significantly to our understanding of the Bible and its contents. The Dead Sea Scrolls have contributed the earliest known copies of books of the Hebrew Bible in whole or in part, as well as pieces of a vast contemporary literature mainly reflecting the interests and the library of the people of Qumrân. All in all, the Dead Sea Scrolls have illuminated the textual history of the Old Testament far beyond any reasonable expectation. They have provided information about and insights into the process by which the Bible came to be, and especially the history of the canon and of the text.

What the discoveries at Qumrân have done for the back end of biblical history, the Ugaritic tablets have helped to do for the front end. Here are a couple of thousand tablets written in a language quite similar to Biblical Hebrew (not counting the many other tablets written in Akkadian and other languages) and dating roughly to the century preceding the career of Moses. The literary texts, including parts of several epics and mythic pieces, constitute the heart and core of the materials found, and are the most important for understanding the linguistic forms and meanings, literary connections and allusions of much biblical poetry. This chance find (quite literally meant since the initial discovery was largely an accident) has proved invaluable for the study of the biblical text, especially biblical poetry.

We should add here as well the inscriptional discoveries at Quntillet Ajrud (ca. 800 B.C.) and at Deir 'Allā (ca. 700 B.C.), and the ostraca from Arad and Beer-sheba (as well as a few others from various sites), which have shed light on the history of the Hebrew language, and especially on a number of passages in the Bible. None of these has proved to be a "smoking pistol," decisive confirmation of, or confrontation with specific biblical people or events. But the illumination and elucidation of difficult passages place us all under obligation to the discoverers and to those who have studied and published the texts.

In the end, the archaeological materials help to illuminate and illustrate, and always to remind us that behind and beyond the pages of Scripture, the history of Israel was lived out by real people in real situations, and that events took place under specified circumstances. Except in unusual and extraordinary cases, archaeology provides only representative artifacts and peripheral data. Even when there are specific points of contact and direct confirmation, the heart and core of the biblical narrative will remain inaccessible to archaeology. The central and decisive components of the biblical account are unique and unrepeatable occurrences inextricably bound up with the divine initiative and action. This dimension of ultimate reality inevitably transcends ordinary historical experience, which limits and defines the boundary of archaeological data.

So however and whatever archaeology contributes to the biblical picture, it is no substitute for faith, no alternative to belief, only a possible help along the way. Probably Albright was fully aware of all this, and had limited expectations. The results of archaeological research were not intended to initiate faith or create belief, but rather to bolster the convictions of those already persuaded, and whose confidence in the face of criticism and skepticism needed to be strengthened. In the end, however, the same dilemmas and difficulties remain.

We may conclude these remarks by reminding ourselves that Albright was not solely interested in maintaining or sustaining the historicity of the biblical account through archaeological research, but rather was concerned with a larger picture, the successful emergence of monotheism as the dominant religion in western civilization. He wished to show how, as well as when and where and under whose inspiration and guidance, monotheism--of the biblical kind--came to be, and how it overcame its natural enemies to become the primary religion of the Western world. He made the presentation not only in historical terms as a kind of evolution from primitive religion through various stages to ethical monotheism, but also in conceptual and theoretical terms to show that such an evolution was actually from lower to higher forms of religion, and that the final stage, reflecting the combination of biblical religion with Greek thought, was the culmination of a very long process.

From the point of view of comparative religion, especially in terms of social science patterns and models, the success of monotheism, especially in its Christian forms, makes an appealing and impressive story, a necessary and essential one in describing the overall human experience. But in the light of 20th century developments and the impact of the major religions upon one another all over the world, it may be that some new synthesis, some new product of the interaction between East and West, between Christianity and its Western companions on the one hand, and Buddhism and its Eastern associates on the other, will result. Albright was rather scornful of such ideas and criticized Toynbee especially for suggesting that some combination of liberal Christianity and Mahayana Buddhism might be the religion, or at least the direction, of the future. It is difficult to predict, and a merger based on least common denominators would hardly represent progress. Nevertheless it is equally hard to believe that the only purpose or function of non-Christian religions in the scheme of things is to serve as false options and blind alleys, only to be displaced and superseded by the triumphant church. Surely a better and more inclusive script must be written for the centuries to come.

A postscript may also be in order--concerning the relationship between the historical and literary dimensions of the biblical tradition and religion. Certainly Albright was right in resisting the non- or anti-historical tendencies in the critical left wing of scholarship. Difficult as it may be to establish, maintain, and defend the historicity of the biblical experience, it is necessary to undertake this task resolutely and without either claiming too much or giving everything away. It cannot be an article of faith exempt from scrutiny, nor can it be merely the historicity of the affirmation or affirming community; believing in belief and affirming affirmation may be the form of religion, but its substance requires historical action and occurrence, the reality of what is affirmed and attested. Albright, in the pursuit of such historical reality, did not neglect the literary form in which the tradition was packaged, but he was interested in results and products, not in the literary character of the material or quality for its own sake. Here perhaps we can make a suggestion that the order of priorities should be reversed or at least balanced.

In my judgment the Bible is first of all literature, and it can only be understood as such, not that we should neglect or abandon the historical component, but that we should recognize the priority of the literary aspect. Albright was rightly skeptical of the several social sciences in their attempts to analyze, interpret, and explain biblical phenomena. The follies and fallacies of Freudian, Darwinian, and Marxian approaches to the Bible have been self-evident. But there are difficulties with the historical-archaeological approach as well, just as there are with theological-philosophical ones. All have their place and can perform their services. But the primary category is perforce the literary one. That is where we must begin, and when we have run the gamut of all the others, that is also where we must end: by which we mean that the literary category is basic and final, and the proper one by which to embrace and encompass, not exclude, the others.

References

Albright, W.F.
  1932   *The Archaeology of Palestine and the Bible*. New York: Revell.

  1940   *From the Stone Age to Christianity*: Monotheism and the Historical
          Process. Baltimore:Johns Hopkins Press.

  1942   *Archaeology and the Religion of Israel*. Baltimore:Johns Hopkins
          Press.

  1968   *Yahweh and the Gods of Canaan*. London:Athlone.

  1972   "Neglected Factors in the Greek Intellectual Revolution," *Proceed-

          ings of the American Philosophical Society* 116.3:225-242.

William F. Albright as a Philologian

Delbert R. Hillers

The Johns Hopkins University

Before reading my paper, I am compelled to say this. Frank Cross jokingly referred to Noel Freedman's having stolen something from him in his paper. I would like to complain that he has pillaged and looted from the field that I am supposed to be talking about so that you will not need to be exceptionally alert to notice that large fields that I speak about have already been touched on by Professor Cross. However, seriously, I feel that this is not a real disadvantage. If we happen to agree in our views, this will be reassuring to you. If we happen to disagree, this may be interesting. So, we'll see about that.

The overlap arises because philology is an extremely broad area of humanistic inquiry and its boundaries are not well defined. In a case like this where precise scientific delimitation of the field is not available, we may turn for a rough-and-ready definition to Webster's Dictionary, where "philology" is said to mean: "the study of literature and relevant disciplines; historical and comparative linguistics; the study of human speech, especially as the vehicle of literature and as a field of study that sheds light on cultural history." Compare this definition from the large Random House lexicon: Philology is said to be "...the study of written records, the establishment of their authenticity and their original form, and the determination of their meaning."

As if these boundaries were not broad enough, William F. Albright was no respecter of boundaries. I note the following brief article that appeared in the *Bulletin of the American Schools of Oriental Research* in 1936, entitled "The Song of Deborah in the Light of Archaeology": Philology is linked with excavation! The same linking manifested itself in reverse in a seminar with Albright during my student days. He told us that he had encountered difficulties in interpreting the relation of certain floors at Tell Beit Mirsim to a particular set of walls. The floors should have gone together with these walls, but were lower than the foundation course! How could this be accounted for? Beaming, Albright looked around the room to see if any one of us had tumbled to the explanation. None of us had. "I had forgotten the Odyssey," Albright explained, and he went on to point out that after Odysseus had slain all the suitors, they of course had to clean up the mess, and *scraped the floors* (Odyssey:22.454-456). This would have *lowered* the level of the earthen floors, the opposite of the usual buildup. In retrospect, I find this much more ingenious than convincing, but perhaps it makes my point about Albright. He loved to combine, not to say drag together, disparate fields of scholarly endeavor, so that to lecture on his attainments as a philologian is made even harder.

Today, however, I will let Albright's disrespect for academic pigeonholes work for me. I am resolved not to be especially concerned about rigidly separating out his philological activity from other interests of his, and covering it comprehensively. I will simply pick out the following four areas that seem to call for comment: First, his decipherment of the Proto-Sinaitic inscriptions; secondly, his vocalization of Egyptian syllabic orthography; third, his work on Ugaritic; and fourth, his studies of early Hebrew poetry.

While I will make some attempt to offer my own assessment of his work on these subjects, I will have as my principal goal to give an account of how his views have been received, and to give a reasoned guess as to how and in what manner his influence may survive. Given the nature of this gathering, I will allow myself to be more personal and anecdotal than might be appropriate in a more strictly academic and stuffy setting. In working through some of Albright's publications again, I am not surprisingly left with this dominant impression of William F. Albright as a philologian. He exemplifies the attempt by a humanist to use scientific method, but in an imaginative way, and similarly, he shows extraordinary ability at imaginative joining of disparate areas of inquiry.

Those of us who knew Albright in his full maturity as a scholar, or in his later years as an elder statesman of incredible reputation, had trouble thinking of him as a student. One felt that he must always have been the way he was in middle life or in old age, and this was only strengthened by the stories of Albright as a self-taught scholar, one who sprang fully grown from Chile and the American Midwest. But though it is true that Albright taught himself Hebrew, Akkadian, and ancient history, he cheerfully admitted that when he arrived at Johns Hopkins to undertake graduate study, "there were some seams showing." In fact, Albright had a disciplined, formal, and rigorous training as a philologian under the foremost scholar in America in this field, Paul Haupt.

Albright told us how in his student days Professor Haupt would, as a regular assignment, make his little group of graduate fellows translate Hebrew psalms into Arabic, Syriac, Akkadian and Sumerian. "The Sumerian was a little wooden," Albright would say somewhat apologetically. In the last years of Albright's teaching, the atmosphere in his seminars and classes in history and archaeology was extremely relaxed and rather disorderly. In my experience, however, Akkadian class was different, and I have since come to understand this as a reflection of his own no-nonsense training in this field.

Perhaps another anecdote is revealing of Albright's attitudes in the area of philological correctness and exactness. In the days when I worked with Albright as editor, a young scholar submitted an article for the *Bulletin of the American Schools of Oriental Research* involving extensive quotation of Akkadian, and, in looking it over for Albright, Herbert Huffmon, then his assistant, discovered a number of little errors in transliterating the Akkadian. He pointed this out to Albright, who commented simply, "Schlechte Kinderstube." This is a largely untranslatable German expression meaning that the scholar in question had not been brought up properly in his childhood days of cuneiform study. No one could say that of Albright. He had a thorough and long academic training as a philologian.

Turning now from Albright's training to his achievements, we begin with a very fundamental level of philological study of texts, namely with decipherment of an unknown script. One of Albright's principal efforts along this line concerned the very early alphabetic inscriptions from Serâbît el-Khâdem in the Sinai peninsula, known as the Proto-Sinaitic inscriptions. The first specimen of this type of writing came to light in the middle of the 19th century, but a sizeable body became known only in 1905 through the work of Sir Flinders Petrie, who correctly concluded from the restricted number of signs that this must be an alphabetic script. In 1915, Sir Alan Gardiner published a partial decipherment; though he claimed to understand only nine out of about 27 signs, they resulted in readings of some groups of characters in a way that has remained convincing, thus, *l-b'lt*, "to Ba'alath." He supported his decipherment by the hypothesis that the script involved use of the acrophonic principle, i.e., the signs were pictures of objects, and stood for the first consonant sound of the name of the object; thus, we have a schematic picture of water (*mayim* or its archaic equivalent), and this design stood for the sound "*m*".

Beginning about 1935, Albright made attempts to complete this decipherment, building on what Gardiner had done. In 1948, he published a relatively complete decipherment--19 characters are interpreted--(Albright 1948:6-22); he filled this out and brought it up to date in a small monograph (Albright 1966).

Though these inscriptions are not especially rich in content, they are nearly our earliest alphabetic inscriptions; Albright dated them to about 1550 to 1450 B.C. They are thus of enormous humanistic interest. The decipherment by Gardiner and Albright has served as a foundation for studies of Frank Cross on the early history of the alphabet, beginning already in 1954 (Cross 1954:15-24) and continuing through a series of publications, notably advancing this field of study, and confirming the general line of thought represented by Albright. Among the texts discovered at ancient Ugarit was one giving in parallel the signs of the Ugaritic alphabet and corresponding syllabic cuneiform signs providing the pronunciation of the first syllable, as in: *g* : *ga* - for *gamlu* "throwstick." This most welcome addition to our knowledge of the names of the letters and their history was studied by Cross and another of Albright's students, Thomas O. Lambdin (Cross and Lambdin 1960:21-26), who concluded that this new text provides "confirmation of other evidence that the names of the Proto-Canaanite signs as well as their order are at least as old as the 14th century B.C., and adds additional support to the view that the acrophonic principle, integral to the names of the signs, went back to the invention of the script."

This is an excellent illustration of Albright's creative ability as a philologian and teacher, and there is little doubt in my mind that Albright is in this case, to use a phrase he was fond of, "right in principle." If I have some reservation, it arises from dissatisfaction with what his Proto-Sinaitic inscriptions *say*. Ancient texts commonly run as much to form as our postcard, "Having fine time, wish you were here." There are Ugaritic letters that consist of practically nothing but formulas, e.g., *KTU 2.24 = PRU 2.14; KTU 2.68 = RS 20.199* (*KTU*, see Dietrich et al 1976). Paradoxically, a decipherer would be reassured if his texts turn out to say commonplace things, for it would show that he is on the right track. But how about "Swear to give a sacrifice in order that we may sacrifice to Baalath" (No. 345), or "'Itha', son of Tsur, give me an oracle. Thou didst save me from two lio[nesses, gr]ant me a r[esting place(?)...]" (No. 352), or (most unexpectedly) "Thou, O Shaphan, collect from 'Ababa eight (?) minas (of turquoise)" (No. 357)? Do we expect to find this kind of thing carved on rock? Long after Albright had retired, I invited him to speak to our Seminar at Hopkins to give students who were born out of due time some experience of him as a teacher. He spoke about the Proto-Sinaitic inscriptions, and I questioned him about the frequent imperatives he found there. About all that he said was: "Yes, there are a lot," obviously unwilling to take my implied objection seriously. All the same, I am left in the odd position of accepting his values for many of the letters and doubting the resulting readings of the texts.

In view of his achievements in other fields, it is easy to forget that Albright studied Egyptian and wrote enough in that field to call for assessment of his achievement. In describing and evaluating his work, I am, of course, wholly dependent on his own statements and the judgments of Egyptologists, but his principal contribution is of exceptional potential interest also for Hebraists.

Ancient Egyptian writing represents vowels not at all, or only most incompletely, and the latest stage of the language, Coptic, can be used only with the greatest difficulty as a resource for reconstructing the pronunciation of older stages. The recovery of the vocalization of various sorts of Egyptian writing, then, was the sort of challenging subject that might have been expected to attract Albright's energies and skills in his younger days.

According to Gardiner's famous *Egyptian Grammar* Appendix A (1957:433), the authority on the vocalization of Middle Egyptian is Sethe, in his work on the Egyptian verb and an article entitled "Die Vocalisation des Ägyptischen" (1923:145-207); in the latter, Sethe also undertook to compare the vocalization of Egyptian to that of the distantly related semitic languages. At this point, Gardiner states: "The conclusions reached by Sethe, though admittedly of a tentative character, coincide on the whole with those of W. F. Albright, whose brief independent study entitled, "*The Principles of Egyp-*

tian Phonological Development," is printed in *Recueil de Travaux*, 40, 64-70."
This sketch, which appeared in 1923, was a digest of a monograph on the
Egyptian vowel system, which was accepted for *Beiträge zur Assyriologie* and
then lost. It had been prepared by Albright during a stay at Johns Hopkins
following his discharge from the Army, when he was in his late 20's (Albright
1964:323).

Albright's Egyptological work that is most widely known, I suppose, is the
Vocalization of the Egyptian Syllabic Orthography, which appeared in 1934
(Albright 1934). It is a short book--only 75 pages--but represents, as Albright
wrote, a great deal of the author's time over a span of seven years. Its
conclusions are almost identical to those presented in a paper on the subject
at an Orientalists Congress in Bonn in 1928 (Sethe *ZDMG* 7:xlv-xlvi).

The Egyptian syllabic orthography is a special system of writing used by
Egyptian scribes beginning perhaps with the New Kingdom, from about 1600
B.C., and continuing through later periods (though the boundaries differ in the
views of various scholars). The signs used are ordinary Egyptian hieroglyphs,
not newly invented signs, but they are written in special groups in a way
distinct from ordinary use. The purpose of this orthography was, in Albright's
formulation, to "...write foreign names and words, as well as rare or ambiguous
Egyptian words and names" (Albright 1934:1). The existence of this peculiar
script as something separate from ordinary hieroglyphs, was first established
by Erman in 1876, and its character debated by Max Müller, Erman, Sethe,
Burchardt, and others in subsequent years. Thus, Albright was by no means
the first to tackle its interpretation, but he felt he could expect success because
of his use of what he called a "purely inductive method," and because of the
presence, at the time of his writing, of three favorable new conditions: the
availability of many more transcriptions of Egyptian words in cuneiform, which
of course indicated approximate vowel sounds; the development of much
better knowledge of West Semitic linguistics; and recent advances in understanding of the vocalization of Middle Egyptian, to which Albright himself, as
we have noted, had already contributed.

With admirable succinctness, Albright reviews the work of his predecessors, then describes his system for interpreting the syllabic orthography. This,
in turn, is supported by a chart giving the value of the syllabic groups, and an
alphabetic list of names and words, mostly Egyptian or Northwest Semitic,
together with Albright's interpretation of their vocalization. The major point
at issue among Egyptologists had been whether the syllabic writing indicated
vowels in any consistent and intelligible way, or only consonants; obviously
Albright comes down on the side of those who held that a real and useful
system of vocalic writing is involved. Egyptological reception of these
conclusions will be presented shortly, but at this point a Semitist may be
permitted to emphasize the potential significance of what might seem a highly
special, technical, and arid field of study.

If correct, Albright is able either to demonstrate for the first time, or to confirm the following major conclusions for Northwest Semitic (Canaanite) of the second millennium B.C., that is--in his playful terminology--for the language of Moses' grandfather: "The Hebrew case-endings were still in use during most of the period under consideration....The Canaanite verbal system...is identical with the corresponding system illustrated by the Canaanite glosses in the Amarna tablets...the accent still fell on the syllable correspond-ing to the accent-syllable in Accadian, and had not yet moved forward to the penult (ultima, if we omit the case-endings)" (Albright 1934:18-20). Out of a host of detailed conclusions concerning the individual words, we may mention only the vocalization *Yardôn* for later Hebrew *Yarden*, and the pronunciation of *Yasir'el*, which Albright believed correct for the second millennium for later *Yisra'el*.

Albright kept up his interest in this subject, bringing out new material in 1954 (1954:222-233). On the evidence of these names, Albright posits that already in the 18th century B.C., Egyptian was "well on the way toward developing an adequate system of indicating vowels in foreign names." In 1957, in a joint paper with his student Thomas O. Lambdin, he added additional material (Albright and Lambdin 1957:113-127). In these same articles he replied to critics of this theory who had in the meantime published their objections.

The most outspoken of these critics was W. F. Edgerton of Chicago, who summed up thus: "It is my considered opinion that no Egyptian scribe of the Nineteenth Dynasty or earlier ever consciously attempted to represent a vowel sound in hieroglyphic or hieratic writing by any device whatever" (Edgerton 1940:506). In the 1957 joint article with Lambdin, Albright scarcely deigns to reply to Edgerton. Others, who may not agree with Albright in all respects, have attempted to find a less extreme position than Edgerton's. Even so, it is hard to see how Edel can really hope for a stance somewhere in the middle between two such diametrically opposed viewpoints (Edel 1948:11-24). It seems most useful to follow out the reaction to Albright's theory by the more sympathetic scholars, Helck and Edel being taken as representatives; in some ways this path leads back to Edgerton, and thus to an impasse.

Wolfgang Helck, in his massive work *Die Beziehungen Ägyptens zu Vorderasien im 3. und 2. Jahrtausend v. Chr.*, makes very extensive reference to Albright's interpretation of the syllabic orthography, and may serve as one means of assessing the validity and influence of Albright's major Egyptological work. A comparison of the table of values for syllabic writings given by Helck (1962:601-602) with that of Albright almost 30 years earlier shows that Helck accepts Albright's values, either exactly or almost exactly, in the great majority of cases. The intervening decades of discovery and discussion result, as might be expected, in numerous additions and modifications, but in essence, Helck adopts both Albright's general position that there is a system of vocalic writing here, and most of the details of interpretation. Helck's work also illustrates the importance of this line of research for understanding Egypt's relation to Syria-Palestine in antiquity. In one respect, however, Helck's extension of Albright's system is disquieting. Albright already reckoned with the existence of a number of polyphonous signs, signs capable of being read with the whole possible repertoire of vocalic values. Thus a certain combination of signs is said to have stood not only for *ma*, but also for *mi* and *mu*. Helck evidently feels that this must be extended, so that he give us an *'a*, which can also be *'i* and *'u*, and other similar cases. There is nothing inherently impossible about this, but if carried too far, it threatens to undermine any "system" involved; to say that *any* vowel may be represented by a group of signs, is another way of saying that *no* vowel is unambiguously represented by that spelling.

This is the point made emphatically by Elmar Edel. As in earlier studies along these lines (Edel 1948:fn4; 1949:44-47), Edel tries to present syllabic orthography as "...eine Mischung von alphabetischer und Silbenschrift," here his study of lists of place-names led him to the positing of new group-writings, and the identification of new ways in which long-known groups had to be read, very much along the lines of Albright. Extension of the earlier system, however, is close to leading to its collapse, in his view. Each new discovery, he points out, leads to additions to the list of syllabic values, with ever higher subscripts such as *'a4*, *'a5* and so on with no foreseeable end. But such a "system" is too complicated to have been practicable, and our transcriptions in the end only veil the fact that most of these groups can stand for all three vowels: *a*, *i*, and *u*. This is the objection stated in sharpest form already by Edgerton, and expressed also by Simons (1937:16-21).

It seems to an outsider that Albright's vocalization is still the leading theory in the sense of being the one under discussion; Helck's treatment does not differ in essentials. But numerous new problems of detail and theory have arisen, serious enough to question the whole attempt. I am not aware that Albright ever really answered the objection that seems to me most serious, that which arises from the polyphony of so many signs. New discoveries may clarify things, of course, but as a scholar, one also learns that while new discoveries sometimes bring "new light," they also almost as often plunge us back into old darkness.

Just at the height of Albright's scholarly career, when he was in his late thirties, cuneiform texts were discovered at Ras Shamra on the Syrian coast, which Albright himself had identified as ancient Ugarit from references in the Amarna letters. Albright had his tiny part in the decipherment, actually achieved, of course, by Bauer, Virolleaud, and Dhorme. Père Edouard Dhorme, in 1930, was working independently on the decipherment of Ugaritic in Jerusalem, on the basis of copies of texts published in Syria by Virolleaud. He had made good progress, but he was still in error on some fundamental points, when he was set straight by Bauer's article in a Berlin newspaper, the *Vossische Zeitung*. This article was transmitted to Dhorme by W. F. Albright, who had it from the archaeologist, Kurt Galling. Albright was, at the time, occupied with the third campaign at Tell Beit Mirsim, and thus had no chance at more than a modest role in the remarkably rapid decipherment of the script that turned out to embody Ugaritic, namely correctly identifying a certain Ugaritic sign as ẓ (Albright 1932:185-208). As it turned out, of course, Albright's main contribution was in the translation and interpretation of the texts. Leaving aside his activity as a student of Canaanite religion, for the most part, I wish now to review his more purely philological preoccupation with Ugaritic texts.

It is impossible to go into detail about Albright's Ugaritic studies, not only because they are numerous, but because in these articles it is often not the case that any major point is being argued, but rather that myriads of philological details are being assembled. I will attempt to summarize in the following generalizations. During the early days of interpretation of the Ugaritic text, Albright was editor of the *Bulletin of the American Schools of Oriental Research*. This gave him an easy means to bring out rapidly the news about Ugaritic studies and to bring out his own contributions to the field. As I reviewed his articles on these ancient Canaanite texts, their nature struck me as somewhat predictable. Here was an immensely learned and brilliant Semitist confronting a body of almost untouched and, in many places, inordinately difficult texts. The result is a mixture of bits that are correct and permanently valuable with others that are at best plausible, and which had only a short life in the discipline. If that judgment is not unfair, it needs to be balanced by recollection of the service rendered by Albright's use of his publications, and his editorial position, to provide a kind of clearinghouse for Ugaritic studies over their earlier years.

Several times in reviewing Albright's philological work, I have used the word "imaginative." Half seriously, I would like to use it again to describe one of the more intriguing titles in our literature, and the brief article devoted to the subject: "Dwarf Craftsmen in the Keret Epic and Elsewhere in North-West Semitic Mythology." Who but Albright could have thought that up; who but Albright would have known that Rabbinic sources tell of dwarfs, one of these little fellows being a rather symmetrical fellow one cubit tall, with a one cubit beard and a penis a cubit and a span long? (Albright 1954:1-4).

To my mind, one of the most durable contributions of Albright to Ugaritic studies--if that is the right adjective--is his treatment of "The Creation of the Composite Bow in Canaanite Mythology," written jointly with his student, George Mendenhall (Albright and Mendenhall 1942:227-229). Significant in itself, it also symbolizes an important aspect of Albright's Ugaritic work and much else that he did: That he was constantly interacting with others, especially his students. I have in my library, as a gift from Professor Albright, his copy of H. L. Ginsberg's *The Legend of King Keret*. Evidently, Albright used this to record his own notes and in teaching, for it is a fantastic palimpsest: Ginsberg's text is overlaid with other translations, readings, vocalizations and interpretations, many of them marked with names in parentheses, thus, such and such a translation (Mendenhall), (Dahood),

(Freedman), (Cross and Freedman). At one interesting point, Albright brackets four lines of Ginsberg's translation, and writes next to them, "all wrong." So Albright was always receiving from others. At the same time, he was also strewing his studies with brief suggestions that his students and others were free to take up. I note from an article on the furniture of El in Canaanite mythology, that Albright, writing on the meter of Ugaritic verse, states (Albright 1943:43): "...the syllable seems to have been counted, since one finds striking agreement" (between parallel cola). Professor Freedman and many others have followed that suggestion out in Ugaritic and Biblical studies.

I will close this section, ungraciously no doubt, with a criticism which forces itself on me in trying to view this aspect of Albright's work in context. In reading Ugaritic texts, Albright surpasses perhaps all others in exploiting broad linguistic and religious knowledge for their interpretation. As a student I was overwhelmed by what the man could bring to bear on a Ugaritic text; reading his work 30 years later, I am still impressed by his knowledge and ingenuity. I also see, or think I see, a danger implicit in his approach, which has manifested itself more in the work of his followers than in his own, and in several directions. On the one side, Albright stressed the connection of Ugaritic to biblical Hebrew language and literature; he did so early, late, and emphatically. If this contributed to the discovery of many a forgotten aspect of ancient Hebrew, it also encouraged a kind of pan-Ugaritism, which by now burdens biblical studies with hundreds of hasty ill-tested suggestions for new words, meanings, or constructions, so that even if one wishes to drop out of this game, it remains necessary to wade through all that has been done, and continues to be done, by those who seem to equate what they imagine to be Ugaritic with Hebrew.

If Albright's work was not without negative effect on biblical studies, this is balanced by some little-recognized damage it did on the Canaanite side. When Albright read Ugaritic religious texts, he had on tap, so to speak, all his knowledge of Phoenician and Punic religion, of what the Bible said about the abominations of the Canaanites, of Philo of Byblos, Damaskios, and much else. The resulting mix is impressive. But one outcome is that in Albright's treatment of Canaanite religion much is blurred; much is attributed by implication to the religion of ancient Ugarit, or to some vague "religion of the Canaanites" that is not attested at Ugarit at all (Hillers 1985:253-269), and certainly not at all times and all places. Prepared as we all are to think the worst of that people whom the Israelites are supposed to have extirpated, Albright did nothing in his work on Ugaritic and Canaanite religion to mitigate the effect of our prejudice.

When I came to study at Johns Hopkins as a full-time graduate student, Albright had me prepare my first seminar paper on the metrical system of Paul Haupt, who was Albright's teacher. This was a very useful exercise for me, though I scarcely thought so as I waded through reams of Haupt's wild, undisciplined dissections and reconstructions of biblical poems, almost entirely forgotten now by scholars. At the least, it eventually helped me to understand Albright a little better, for I believe Haupt inspired his interest in Hebrew poetry on the one hand, and on the other led him to adopt opposing positions. If Haupt dated everything late--in the Maccabean period by preference--Albright looked for evidence of great antiquity; if Haupt frequently cut out as much as 75% of the Massoretic text as inauthentic accretions--glosses, glosses on glosses, and sons of sons of glosses--Albright was infinitely more conservative in textual matters.

(Sometimes, when he felt something was lacking in a Biblical poem, Paul Haupt would compose a stanza and insert it in his text. I do not know that Albright ever did that, although no one could accuse him of lacking confidence.)

I saw Albright most working days during the last part of his life, during the time when he was working on his latest extensive treatment of Hebrew poetry in *Yahweh and the Gods of Canaan* (Albright 1968:22). In reviewing his earlier works on Hebrew verse, I am struck by the continuity in approach and detail, going back to a treatment of the Song of Deborah in 1921 (Albright 1921:69-86), running through his subsequent article on the same poem in 1936 (Albright 1936:26-31), and classic studies of the Balaam oracles (Albright 1944:207-233), "the Song of Habakkuk" (Albright 1946:1-18), Psalm 68 (Albright 1951:1-39), the Song of Moses (Albright 1959: 339-346), and the Song of Songs (Albright 1962:1-7), and the extended treatment of "Verse and Prose" in *Yahweh and the Gods of Canaan*. It is not only remarkable that Albright kept coming back to the same rather narrow body of poems, but that he kept working at a refining of the same methodological approaches. Thus, already in the 1936 article, we find emphasis on the use of linguistic information from Ugaritic, exploited to explain the use of *'az* and *zeh sinay* ("the One of Sinai"). Already in the article on the Balaam oracles, Albright is concerned with the importance of the "original orthography" for the date and interpretation of the poems; this is in 1944, an era we may think of in this connection, and in this company, as "pre-Cross and Freedman," since their developed study of Hebrew orthography appeared only in 1952. Along with much else, the "Song of Habakkuk" study emphasizes the distinction between archaic and archaizing. The footnotes to "Psalm 68" make it plain that by then (1950-51), Albright had set his students on this profitable path of research; the article itself shows Albright concerned with typological dating of early Hebrew verse in an increasingly refined way, arguing from a distinction between climactic and repetitive parallelism. Albright frankly credits several of the emendations he adopts to "my student, Dr. Samuel Iwry." (I assume that Dr. Iwry was gratified by this acceptance; in later years, I experienced it several times, and I felt that it was like having one's name written in the Book of Life.) In the treatment of points in the Song of Moses (Deut. 32), we find a combination of Ugaritic resources with readings in one of the Dead Sea Scroll Fragments. The Song of Songs article brings us, to select a few items, remarks on numerical gradation (60 and 80 in parallel), asseverative *kî, le* for *m*, and sequence dating of poetry in more developed form.

It is not my intention to claim that in all these exciting philological discoveries, Albright always could claim absolute primacy, though in some cases he could. It is clear that he was always in the forefront; clear, too, that the work of Dahood and Cross and Freedman--and their students, in turn--is intertwined with his and grows out of it. I have referred sometimes facetiously to Albright's combination of archaeological data with philological matters. In treating Hebrew verse, we see Albright applying archaeology at a deeper level, the level of methodology. Frank Cross has written of Albright as a master of typological method (Cross 1970:7-11). Whatever new evidence may bring to light bearing on the chronology of repetitive parallelism versus other types, Albright will surely prove to have been on the right track methodologically.

If I may briefly state several criticisms, I note that in contrast to Haupt, Albright was conservative in his treatment of the Massoretic text. He seems to have passed this on to his students. Indeed, I suppose that all of us closely under Albright's influence shared his characteristic attitude and are grateful for it. But in some, this conservatism has taken the form of an unwillingness to admit any error in the text or to allow any role to scholarly conjecture in its restoration. While granting that this, as a methodological approach, is fruitful in many cases, I must observe that it is open to many objections. Lacking time here to go into them, I will content myself with saying that this was not really Albright's own attitude, for he was much more eclectic and free. The late Monsignor Patrick Skehan once read at a small biblical conference a paper, subsequently published (Skehan 1971:27-45), in which he attempted to show the presence of an elaborate structure in the early chapters of Proverbs, based on numerical ratios between its parts. Albright's reaction at the time, whatever its cogency as a criticism of Skehan's view, was at least characteristic of Albright's own common-sense view of textual matters. Albright said he did not see how the text of Proverbs could possibly have been transmitted in the pristine shape demanded by Skehan's theory, in the light of what we know about the transmission of other ancient texts, which are always suffering losses and distortions in transmission.

To sum up this section and conclude my remarks, it is my opinion that here Albright did perhaps his most influential and permanent philological work, inaugurating lines of research which are not yet exhausted, in spite of the many followers whom he has set working.

References

Albright, W. F.

1921 "The Earliest Forms of Hebrew Verse," *Journal of the Palestine Oriental Society* 2:69-86.

1932 "The North-Canaanite Epic of 'Alêyân Ba'al and Môt," *Journal of the Palestine Oriental Society* 12:185-208.

1934 *The Vocalization of the Egyptian Syllabic Orthography*. American Oriental Series 5. New Haven.

1936 "The Song of Deborah in the Light of Archaeology," *Bulletin of the American Schools of Oriental Research* 62: 26-31.

1943 "The Furniture of El in Canaanite Mythology," *Bulletin of the American Schools of Oriental Research* 91:39-44.

1944 "The Oracles of Balaam," *Journal of Biblical Literature* 63:207-233.

1946 "The Song of Habakkuk," in *Studies in Old Testament Prophecy* (ed. H. H. Rowley). Edinburgh:T. & T. Clark.1-18.

1948 "The Early Alphabetic Inscriptions from Sinai and Their Decipherment," *Bulletin of the American Schools of Oriental Research* 110:6-22.

1951 "A Catalogue of Early Hebrew Lyric Poems (Psalm LXVIII)," *Hebrew Union College Annual* 23:1, 1-39.

1954 "Northwest-Semitic Names in a List of Egyptian Slaves from the Eighteenth Century B.C.," *Journal of the American Oriental Society* 74:222-233.

1954   "Dwarf Craftsmen in the Keret Epic and Elsewhere in North-West Semitic Mythology," *Israel Exploration Journal* 4:1-4.

1959   "Some Remarks on the Song of Moses in Deuteronomy XXXII," *Vetus Testamentum* 9:339-346.

1962   "Archaic Survivals in the Text of Canticles," in *Hebrew and Semitic Studies presented to Godfrey Rolles Driver*. Oxford:University Press. 1-7.

1964   *History, Archaeology and Christian Humanism*. New York:McGraw-Hill.

1966   The Proto-Sinaitic Inscriptions and Their Decipherment, *Harvard Theological Studies* XXII. Cambridge:Harvard Press.

1968   *Yahweh and the Gods of Canaan*. London:Athlone.

Albright, W. F. and T. O. Lambdin

1957   "New Material for the Egyptian Syllabic Orthography," *Journal of Semitic Studies* 2:113-127.

Albright, W. F. and G. Mendenhall

1942   "The Creation of the Composite Bow in Canaanite Mythology," *Journal of Near Eastern Studies* 1:227-229.

Cross, F. M.

1954   "The Evolution of the Proto-Canaanite Alphabet," *Bulletin of the American Schools of Oriental Research* 134:15-24.

1970   "William Foxwell Albright: Orientalist," *Bulletin of the American Schools of Oriental Research* 200:7-11.

Cross F. M. and T. O. Lambdin

1960   "A Ugaritic Abecedary and the Origins of the Proto-Canaanite Alphabet," *Bulletin of the American Schools of Oriental Research* 160:21-26.

Dietrich, M., O. Loretz, and J. Sanmartin

1976   *Die Keilalphabetischen Texte aus Ugarit.* Alter Orient und Altes
        Testament, Band 24. Kevelaer:Butzon & Bercker and Neukir-
        chen-Vluyn, Neikirchener.

Edel, E.

1948   "Neue Keilschriftliche Umschreibungen Ägyptischer Namen aus den
        Bogazköytexten," *Journal of Near Eastern Studies* 7:11-24.

1949   "Neues Material zur Beurteilung der syllabischen Orthographie des
        Ägyptischen," *Journal of Near Eastern Studies* 8:44-47.

1966   *Die Ortsnamenlisten aus dem Totentempel Amenophis III.* Bonner
        Biblische Beiträge 25. Bonn:Peter Hanstein.

Edgerton, W. F.

1940   "Egyptian Phonetic Writing, from its Invention to the close of the
        Nineteenth Dynasty," *Journal of the American Oriental Society*
        60:473-506.

Gardiner, Sir Alan

1957   *Egyptian Grammar.* 3rd ed. revised. London:Oxford University.

Ginsberg, H. L.

1946   *The Legend of King Keret.* *Bulletin of the American Schools of
        Oriental Research.* *Supplementary Studies* 2-3. New Haven:American
        Schools of Oriental Research.

Helck, W.

1962   *Die Beziehungen Ägyptens zu Vorderasien im 3. und 2. Jahrtausend
        v. Chr.* Wiesbaden:Harrassowitz.

Hillers, D. R.

1985   "Analyzing the Abominable," *Jewish Quarterly Review* 75:253-269.

Sethe, K.

  1923   "Die Vocalisation des Ägyptischen," *Zeitschrift der Deutschen Morgenlandischen Gesellschaft* 77:145-207.

Simons SJ, J.

  1937   *Handbook for the Study of Egyptian Topographical Lists Relating to Western Asia*. 16-21. Leiden:Brill.

Skehan, P. W.

  1971   "Wisdom's House," in *Studies in Israelite Poetry and Wisdom*. Catholic Biblical Quarterly Monograph Series I:27-45. Washington, D.C.:Catholic Biblical Association. Reprinted in revised form from *Catholic Biblical Quarterly* 29 (1967):162-180.

W. F. Albright's Contribution to Archaeology

Gus W. Van Beek

Smithsonian Institution

At the 69th General Meeting of the Archaeological Institute of America in 1967, W.F. Albright was awarded the third gold medal of the Institute for distinguished archaeological achievement. The citation reads in part: "William Foxwell Albright, authority on the archaeology, religions and languages of the Near East, has come close to being the "universal man" of archaeology. ...His pioneer work as an excavator at Tell Beit Mirsim and the systematic study of the pottery found there, nearly forty years ago, resulted in the establishment of the archaeological chronology which is the basis of all work conducted in the Holy Land today. ...His research in many fields--the Canaanites, Hebrew palaeography, the Egyptian syllabic vocabulary, the archaeology of South Arabia--is well-nigh incredible in its variety and depth..." (*American Journal of Archaeology* 72:160). This succinct tribute has monumental proportions in describing Albright as "close to being the universal man of archaeology." Let us examine this proposition in the light of the present status of our knowledge of the history of Near Eastern archaeology, some 13 years after his death.

To say that the archaeology of Palestine was in a poor state when Albright entered the scene in 1920 is an understatement; it was, in fact, confused, chaotic, and hopeless. To be sure, there had been at least 12 soundings and excavations in the land, of which the work by Petrie and Bliss at Tell el-Hesi, Sellin at Taanach, Macalister at Gezer, Schumacher at Megiddo, Sellin and Watzinger at Jericho, and Reisner at Samaria were the largest and most important. Albright's evaluation of the information gained from these and other excavations is to the point: "In spite of the quantity of objects and of data brought to light and made accessible to scholars (by 1913 virtually all pre-War excavations had been published), the results were disappointing and we have not yet entirely recovered from the disillusionment which their publication caused in philological and historical circles. This reaction was due not only to the extremely small proportion of written documents found by Palestinian excavators, but perhaps mainly to the vague and conflicting character of their conclusions" (Albright 1940:55). Elsewhere he noted: "...the net gain in improvement of technique was much greater than the gain in chronology and historical interpretation" (Albright 1949:30).

It was this scene that Albright entered in 1920 as the Thayer Fellow at the American Schools of Oriental Research, Jerusalem. He was scarcely prepared to undertake archaeological research by virtue of his training under Paul Haupt at the Johns Hopkins University with his primary emphasis on

61

Semitic languages and philology. Indeed, Albright's publications between 1920 and 1922 reflected his training and major interests; they centered chiefly on Mesopotamian and Akkadian topics but with a gradual increase in Biblical and Hebrew subjects, and his first articles on archaeology appeared toward the end of the period. While in Jerusalem, he mastered spoken Arabic and Hebrew, studied folklore, and became thoroughly familiar with the topography and archaeological sites of the land. Within this two-year period, Albright visited virtually all parts of Palestine, from Tyre in the north to Gaza in the south, and from the coast to the eastern shores of the Sea of Galilee and the Dead Sea, and even managed his first trip to Egypt. When visiting ancient sites, he did what all archaeologists do: he picked up potsherds from the surface and dated them to determine the occupation periods of the site. He also spent three days working with the British excavators at Ashkelon. Thus, by 1922 when he began to excavate Tell el-Fûl, he had already acquired a first-hand knowledge of the topography of Palestine, a working knowledge--as much as was then known--of characteristic pottery types, and modest experience in excavating.

With a grant of $1000, he undertook several short campaigns at Tell el-Fûl, the results of which were published in 1924 (Albright 1924). In such prompt publication, he rivaled Sir Flinders Petrie! Viewed from our perspective, he conducted a remarkable excavation at Tell el-Fûl. His description of the architectural remains was sound, stressing accuracy in observing details and common sense in determining phases of construction. To describe pottery, he adopted the narrative style of his predecessors, rather than tables with abbreviated data, and he continued to use this style throughout his archaeological career. This narrative style was extraordinarily flexible, permitting him to adapt descriptions to the needs, to emphasize significant features, and to include sometimes lengthy discussions of comparative material from other sites. His survey of the literature bearing on the identification of Tell el-Fûl led him to conclude that it was Gibeah of Saul, an identification now questioned by some scholars. His description of the history of Gibeah of Saul in the light of literary sources and the archaeological data is a model replete with detail and balance.

In 1926, Albright began a series of four field seasons at Tell Beit Mirsim, a site in the Judean hills about 12 miles southwest of Hebron. Before beginning the excavations, he had provisionally identified the site with Kirjath-sepher and Debir, an identification that is also being debated today. The site was a happy choice. Its stratification was comparatively simple, owing to the fact that many of the occupation layers were horizontal, rather than sloping, and were separated by burned layers. Moreover, the sequence of occupations stretched from the late third millennium to the early sixth century B.C. with few gaps, enabling him to build on, and to refine the pottery sequence developed at Tell el-Fûl. At the same time, Tell Beit Mirsim was far more complex than Tell el-Fûl because of its greater size and depth, greater number of structures to sort into building phases and to record in the architectural plans, and greater quantity and variety of artifacts.

The field work and publication of the results occupied most of Albright's time for a decade, with the final reports appearing in four volumes (Albright 1932, 1933, 1938, 1943). Tell Beit Mirsim and Tell el-Fûl were Albright's major archaeological research projects in Palestine, resulting in his greatest contribution to Levantine archaeology: the development of the pottery typology and chronology spanning the second millennium and first half of the first millennium B.C.

He also undertook smaller projects: soundings or exavations at two tumuli at Malhah, at Bâb edh-Dhrâ', at Deir Ghassaneh, and at Ader. He served as archaeological director for both Ovid R. Seller's excavations at Beth-zur, and of James L. Kelso's excavations at Bethel, each for one season. Disturbances in Palestine in the 1930's and the advent of World War II ended Albright's excavating career in Palestine.

Following the War, Albright joined forces--as archaeological direc-tor--with a young promoter and leader of scientific and cultural expeditions, Wendell Phillips. In 1947, they went to Sinai where Albright found a small port site near Merkhah of the 15th century B.C.; he also studied the area around Serâbît el-Khâdem, where the proto-Sinaitic inscriptions had been discovered.

In 1950, Albright and Phillips initiated a series of excavations in southern Arabia, at sites in Wadi Beihân, West Aden Protectorate (now South Yemen), which remain to this day the only large-scale excavations ever undertaken in the southern part of the Arabian peninsula. The sites included three areas at Hajar Kohlan (ancient Timna', the capital of the kingdom of Qatabân), together with the Timna' Cemetery, and a small village site, Hajar Bin Humeid, located some seven miles south of Timna'. Although seriously handicapped by a shortage of trained personnel and field time--only seven weeks were available--astonishing results were obtained. Most important was the discovery of an inscription on a building containing the name of a king, Shahr Yagil Yuhargib, and two other names, 'Aqrabum and Thuwaybum. The latter names also appeared, cast in relief on the bases of two magnificent bronze lions of Hellenistic style found in the debris in front of the building. The linking of these personal names with Shahr Yagil Yuhargib and with a Hellenistic work of art proved that this king had reigned during the Hellenistic period. This discovery forever settled the long debated question regarding the chronology of the South Arabian kings and kingdoms in favor of the low chronology; the advocates of the high chronology had dated the reign of Shahr Yagil Yuhargib in the ninth century B.C., while those who held to the low chronology had placed it in the second or first century B.C.

The following year Albright returned to Beiḥân for a half-season, which was his last archaeological fieldwork. That field season was my first, and for me--then a graduate student--it was a singular honor to serve under my teacher. Because of the number of sites and areas being excavated, he was unable to devote his attention to all aspects of the operations as he had done in Palestine. At Hajar Bin Ḥumeid, for example, we saw him about twice each week and for only an hour or two each visit; for excavation methodology and strategy, we were largely left to our own devices. While the primary objective in the excavation of Hajar Bin Ḥumeid was the development of a pottery chronology for southern Arabia, it is my impression that during the 1950 field season, Albright became disenchanted with the prospects of succeeding because of the paucity of sherds. In the 1951 season, for example, I saved and catalogued about 95% of *all* sherds recovered for a total of only 3,208; in a typical site in Israel or Jordan, the excavation of an area of the same size and volume, would yield at least a hundred times as many sherds. Albright subsequently charged me with the responsibility of developing the pottery chronology. At first, I tried to use traditional Near Eastern ceramic criteria in this task, but these did not work because of the limiting characteristics of the pottery sample. Thereafter, I successfully employed typological categories and seriation techniques modeled after those used in American archaeology. The theory, methodology, and analytical observation required by this effort made it one of the two richest experiences of my career, and to Albright I am forever grateful for that opportunity.

During the last third of the 20th century, innovation has come to rank higher in intellectual activity than perhaps at any other time in human history. As members of this generation, what can we say of Albright's archaeological innovations in summarizing his career? In excavation technique, he was not an innovator. He rigorously applied the accepted methods of his time. Those methods, initiated by the great pioneer, George Reisner, were in some aspects misunderstood, regarded of little importance, or simply rejected by his pupil, Clarence Fisher. But it was Fisher who trained Albright as well as all other American excavators in Palestine during the 1920's and 1930's, and in so doing thwarted the advance in archaeological methodology in Palestine for at least two generations. Fisher's methods focused on the excavation of architectural units--chiefly buildings and rooms--with little or no regard for the surrounding natural layers of debris and their relationship to structures. Many stratigraphic difficulties result from these techniques, often making trustworthy interpretation impossible. For example, walls were frequently defined by trenching along both faces, which destroyed all evidence of the relationship of the walls to surrounding debris layers, including foundation trenches. Even when foundation trenches were not obliterated, they were often missed or ignored by excavators. Yet foundation trenches define the relationship of walls to ground level at the time of construction; without this relationship, walls in tells and other multiperiod sites float vertically in the stratigraphy, and the time of construction cannot be determined with confidence. If foundation trenches are missed, the date of construction and the period of habitation are almost always assigned to an earlier occupation.

Fisher's methodology remained unchanged until 1952, when Kathleen Kenyon--utilizing methods developed by her teacher, Sir R. E. Mortimer Wheeler and his pupils--introduced in the Near East the concept of natural stratigraphy. Accordingly, natural debris layers became the basic unit for analyzing stratification, with a major emphasis on the relationships of layers to structures. Albright recognized the important results of the new methodology. He observed: "...the technique of archaeology has been greatly advanced by the technique of Kathleen Kenyon, building on the foundations laid by Sir Mortimer Wheeler, her teacher in archaeology. Her excavation of Jericho (1952-1958) was in every sense an epoch-making undertaking" (Albright 1964:116). But I am still doubtful if he grasped the fundamental, and indeed revolutionary, principles of the Wheeler-Kenyon approach.

Yet Fisher's type of architectural analysis served Albright rather well, better than most of his contemporaries who also employed these methods, because he rigorously studied walls to ascertain phases of construction and relationships to one another. He observed changing sizes of stones, types of shaping and dressing, bonding practices, and interstitial packings. His text, plans, and photographs explain the successive architectural remains with clarity and logic. Albright relied heavily on pottery contexts for his architectural analysis, more so than we do today. He noted in *Tell Beit Mirsim*: "...we should have repeatedly found ourselves at a loss and have made wrong analyses and attributions if it had not been for the precision with which we used the pottery criterion. Here my many years of intensive study of Palestinian pottery bore fruit. All problems of the attribution of walls to accompanying strata were attacked by considering the pottery context above adjacent floor-levels, below such floors, under foundations, in walls which were being broken up for the purpose of clearing away an excavated stratum, etc." (Albright 1938:para. 13).

Nor was Albright an innovator in the development of broad-scale environmental studies, which are increasingly important concerns of Near Eastern archaeologists today. The utilization of geological, floral, faunal, and ethnographical data from the site and its surroundings for a fuller understanding of the environment--its potential and limitations--and of man's imaginative use of that environment apparently aroused only a slight interest in Albright. He did obtain identification of wood samples from Tell el-Fûl, and he noted that the species of tree from which the sample came no longer grows in the area. For Tell Beit Mirsim, he gave a short description of its topographic setting and of other sites in the vicinity. He noted that the type of rock in the district "...is Cretaceous limestone of various types and ages." He briefly discussed water resources, stating that there were subterranean pockets and basins of water under some of the wadies that made permanent settlements possible. During one season (1930), Ovid Sellers kept a temperature log with daily comments on the weather for a period of 51 days (Albright 1938:para. 4). In a single paragraph, Albright discussed the marginal agricultural conditions around the site, noting that the area could expect a good harvest every other year normally, that the area was not suitable for viticulture but might be for olives although none were growing there at the time, and that spring vegetables did well in good seasons. He pointed out that the area was excellent for raising sheep and goats, and that "...It is, therefore, not surprising that the principal industry of the town in the time of stratum A was the weaving and dyeing of woolen cloth" (Albright 1938:para. 6). But significant questions about minor climate fluctuations and human subsistence strategies as indicated by floral and faunal remains in the site never figured among his research interests nor, for that matter, among those of his contemporaries. These were research areas for the future in Israel, and the first projects to address these concerns systematically and rigorously began there in 1970.

Yet Albright correctly foresaw future developments in both archaeological techniques and environmental concerns, and the consequences of those developments. In his presidential address to the American Oriental Society, April 15, 1936, he was prophetic in saying: "We may rest assured that, in coming years, archaeological method will become more and more refined, so that the amount excavated with a given sum of money will progressively dwindle, and the relative importance of the results obtained in a given area or volume will steadily increase. The importance of chemical, geological, and biological methods...is certain to become greater as time goes on" (Albright 1964:116).

Albright's most significant innovations are to be found in his analyses of man-made artifacts recovered from excavations, especially pottery. In this area of research, he stood head and shoulders above his peers, Fisher, Petrie, Garstang, Guy, Loud, Shipton, McCown, and Starkey. To the creation and refining of relative and absolute chronologies of pottery, he brought the full resources of his analytical mind, and his keen powers of observation, tempered with his extraordinary common sense, all distinguishing traits of a master typologist. The major focus of his activity was, of course, the pottery of Palestine, with its obvious correlates throughout the Levant. His expertise, however, reached into the pottery chronologies of other cultures, from the Aegean to South Arabia and from Mesopotamia to Egypt, to which he made important contributions. Chiefly focusing on homogeneous loci in the excavations--such sealed deposits as pits, silos, and rooms--Albright selected representative sherds, which he classified according to shape, especially rim profile, handle form, and base, together with the methods of finishing and decoration. Whole pots and selected sherds were carefully drawn to scale; the remaining sherds were photographed. All were described far more completely than by any previous excavator, and the quality of his descriptions are seldom if ever exceeded today. He also systematically compared types of pottery with those from other sites that had already been published or that he had seen, and these discussions, most of which were relegated to lengthy footnotes, often contain insightful arguments for redating occupation periods elsewhere. The unstructured flow of information inherent in his narrative presentation easily accommodated these wide-ranging discussions, elaborations, and subtle distinctions. One example from Tell Beit Mirsim will suffice: "The large, shallow bowls with inverted rims continue as a category through the entire C (LB II) period, but the technique is so different in detail that it is seldom hard to distinguish a rim of period D (late MB II) from a C rim...This type of bowl attains its greatest popularity in period C; in B (Iron I) the inverted rim disappears completely, as elsewhere in southern and central Palestine during the EI I, so the inverted rim forms a solid criterion for distinguishing Bronze from Iron Age pottery" (Albright 1932:para. 53).

His analyses and publications of pottery were of the greatest benefit not only to professional archaeologists but also to students. As a Fellow at the American School of Oriental Research in Jerusalem (now the Albright Institute of Archaeological Research), I recall finding the actual sherds used in the illustrations of the Tell Beit Mirsim volumes neatly numbered and stored in shoeboxes--one shoebox per half-plate or plate--in the attic of the School in 1952. I spent much of my free time studying these sherds together with the text and plates of the Tell Beit Mirsim volumes to learn the finer, more detailed characteristics of Bronze and Iron Age pottery.

Thus Albright's intensive study of the pottery from dependable contexts enabled him to develop the pottery chronology for Palestine and, with minor regional changes, for the neighboring Levantine countries; this chronology remains the basic framework for all archaeology in these countries today. This was his major contribution to Near Eastern archaeology. In the dedication of the W. F. Albright Volume in the *Eretz Israel* series, the late Yigael Yadin wrote: "Albright's work as an excavator is a classic illustration of the maxim that it is not the sensational aspects of the finds which set the tone and significance of the dig. His excavation at Tell Beit Mirsim yielded a meagre harvest of finds, but his publications which set forth the results of the dig became the foundation of Holy Land archaeology. In them he expounded the theory of archaeology in such a fundamental way that no excavator since has been able to match his achievement" (Yadin 1969:x-xi).

I think the primary motivation for Albright's archaeological research was the recovery of data that would be useful for chronological and historical reconstruction. That is to say, for him archaeological investigation was a means to an end; it was not archaeology for the sake of archaeology as a discipline, or for the fun of excavating. In Palestine, he sought to relate the full range of site events and artifacts to the Bible, and the success of this process vastly increased confidence in the substantial historicity of much of the Bible at a time when Wellhausenian onslaughts--however well meaning--had shredded the confidence of biblical scholars, their colleagues specializing in other ancient literatures, and many of the learned laity. In South Arabia, he sought and found the data necessary to resolve the basic chronological problem and related historical issues.

Albright was also a master in merging archaeological, linguistic, and philological data to reconstruct cultural history. No other scholar of his time or of our time controlled so many of the diverse streams of information flowing from the disciplines of archaeology, languages, and literatures of the Near East, and managed so successfully to unite these streams to form a mighty river. Integrating information from these disciplines, Albright developed a holistic view of the cultures of the ancient Near East, addressing not only walls and pots, but also the full range of political and cultural histories, technological triumphs and intellectual achievements. The synthesis thus created became an independent structure that, in turn, paradoxically enhanced its parts. It gave new meanings to the basic data and produced additional fresh insights with varying degrees of probability.

He generally subjected his ideas and conclusions to rigorous examination, and he frequently revised his ideas as new evidence came to light. At Tell Beit Mirsim, for example, he reassigned the first casemate wall to stratum B phase 3 (10th century B.C.),instead of stratum B phase 1 (12th century), after discoveries in subsequent field seasons shed new light on the relationship of walls. But his intuitive sense of the probable in historical development sometimes led him to make associations only marginally suggested by the data. With the passage of time, some of these tantalizing, tentative associations ascended the scale of probability until they became virtually certain. The process stemmed, I think, from an enthusiasm for and total immersion in the process of historical reconstruction and synthesis. But in all fairness, we must admit that it sometimes resulted from lapses in reappraising premises and reexamining evidence. All of his students and most of his colleagues were familiar with this process, and developed mental filters to strain out obvious exaggerations.

Thus the basis for major criticisms of Albright's scholarship in archaeology is that he overinterpreted evidence and let his hypothetical constructs get out of hand. Clearly this criticism is justified in some instances, but occasionally the criticisms and the alternatives proposed by critics are flawed for the very same reasons.

Let me cite an example. There have been challenges to Albright's use of archaeological and biblical data to reconstruct the Israelite conquest of Canaan in the 13th century B.C., which have been succinctly discussed by Miller (1979:38-40). Albright held that Tell Beit Mirsim and Lachish were destroyed about 1230 B.C., while Bethel and Jericho were destroyed no later than the early 13th century. Subsequently, Hazor was added to the list (1949:108-109). This conclusion rested on the occurrence of burning--represented by a substantial ashy layer--between the latest clear Late Bronze II and the Iron I occupation periods. The "burnings" were interpreted as destructions resulting from the Israelite conquest. In taking issue with Albright's reconstruction, Miller listed the towns mentioned in the biblical account of the conquest that have now been excavated, and that show either (1) no 13th century occupation at all--Arad, Hormah, Heshbon, Jericho, Ai, Gibeon, and Jarmuth--or (2) no evidence of a destruction at that time--Jerusalem and Hebron. This led Miller to suggest that "...archaeology does not provide determinative evidence for dating and/or clarifying the process by which the Israelites gained possession of Canaan" (1979:40). In this controversy both Albright and Miller are wrong because their basic assumptions regarding the meaning of the archaeological evidence, or lack of it, are fallacious. These assumptions are: (1) The occurrence of "burning," i.e., a substantial ashy layer and traces of burning on associated walls and artifacts, represents a *destruction*, and (2) in the absence of evidence to the contrary, all destructions are the result of *warfare*.

Let us briefly examine these assumptions. It should be obvious to all archaeologists and historians that even substantial ash deposits may reflect any of a number of possible activities and events. The most obvious ash-producing activities--those responsible for most thick deposits--are industrial activities that consume vast quantities of fuel and produce enormous ash deposits: ceramic kilns, lime-burning kilns, and metallurgical operations. Even simple bread ovens found in virtually every open courtyard produce ash layers as much as 12 inches thick and sometimes extending 20 feet from the oven.

But there were also many other possible causes of burning. Accidental fires surely occurred in houses and other buildings as a result of cooking fires, children playing with fire, wind-blown embers from the burning-off of fields, and fires following major or minor earthquakes, which occur frequently in Palestine. Deliberate fires must have been set often to destroy an unwanted structure in clearing a building site, or in the course of personal or family vendettas. Obviously the causes of ash layers in sites are legion; not all represent intentional destructive activity, and of those that do, not all can be attributed to invasion and conquest. Yet Albright, Miller, and most other Near Eastern archaeologists excavating today automatically assume that a substantial--and often even a small--ash deposit is evidence of warfare, and immediately seek to associate it with an invasion mentioned in a biblical or other historical text.

One can only conclude that an occupation has been destroyed in warfare *if there is clear evidence of military activity*; fire and ash layers by themselves are not sufficient, and to accept them as such is uncritical interpretation. Documentation in text, representation in art, and the recovery of a number of specialized artifacts such as arrow-heads or spearpoints, fragments of armor, missiles, fallen bodies, evidence of a battering ram or its activities, or a sapper's tunnel are essential to prove that a battle took place. No one can argue with the combination of text, art, site and artifact evidence for Sennacherib's conquest of Lachish, or even without art evidence, for the Roman conquest of Masada.

In the absence of firm textual or representational support, the prospects of finding definitive evidence of warfare or war damage on a site are slim indeed. Most excavations only sample the site, and the samples are so very small that finding the type of artifactual evidence listed above would be astonishing luck. At Tell Jemmeh, for example, in the last phase of the LB II occupation of the 13th century B.C.--the period in which we dug the largest area of the site in terms of square meters--we only excavated 1.67% of the tell. With such a small portion of the site cleared, it would have been most surprising if we had found any of these indications of warfare. We did find an enormous ash layer in our principal area, but it was clearly industrial waste, and in other areas, the only ash encountered came from bread ovens. Does this mean that Tell Jemmeh was not conquered in a military action at the end of the 13th century? Not at all. Somewhere in the remaining 98.33% of the site there may well be a section of the city wall smashed, or a city gate destroyed, contorted skeletons, or the accouterments of battle to establish-beyond doubt that the town had fallen in an attack. Our present information is simply not sufficient to address the question of destruction by warfare, and until more data are forthcoming, the question of conquest must be held in abeyance. What is true of Jemmeh, is true of every other 13th century site in Israel. We rarely have unequivocal evidence of warfare on the one hand, and not enough of any site has been excavated on the other hand, to consider the issue of the Israelite conquest; the question is both inappropriate and untimely until much more evidence is obtained. Ultimately, I think this question will be resolved. What is needed immediately is a major research program to analyze ash samples from all types of deposits and to build a data base of these analyses, so that we may be able to differentiate between the types and sources of ash layers in sites. We also need another 300-400 years of *quality* excavation in relevant sites if we are to get sufficient data to shed light on the Israelite conquest. In any case, Albright, Miller, and others have misused the archaeological evidence in arguing the question.

Each of Albright's major historical interpretations of archaeological data is being weighed in the balance. Some few--such as the one we have discussed above--may be found wanting, although as we have seen, it is much too soon to form a conclusion. Others--such as the substantial abandonment of Judea following the Babylonian conquest, or his date for the effective domestication of the camel and its introduction into the Levant--will almost surely be validated by this generation. Albright refused to take a nihilistic approach in his studies of ancient man and culture. He preferred to accept the essential historicity of documents until proven wrong, and he marshalled his vast and unparalleled knowledge of languages, literatures, and archaeology to measure that historicity. If he erred in this task, it was on the positive rather than the negative side. As an archaeologist who is now more than 30 years out of Albright's classroom, I believe wholeheartedly in his approach; our research must lead to an increase in trustworthy data, to a dispassionate, critical examination of these data, and to the interpretation of data in broad--sometimes daring--ways as we frame our tentative reconstructions of human culture and history, knowing that those reconstructions may eventually be largely recast or discarded altogether.

However in reviewing Albright's archaeological career, I am more convinced than ever that his most *lasting* contributions to scholarship--and, for that matter, ours also--are not to be found in the realm of historical and anthropological theory, or broad-scale interpretations, but rather in the area of full and accurate descriptive studies, e.g., pottery typologies and chronologies, palaeographic typologies, decipherment, text translation, etc. Such studies are the solid building blocks of the edifice of knowledge and truth. Albright bequeathed an enormous amount of descriptive archaeological data, primarily for the cultural history of the Levant and southern Arabia. Because of his wide-ranging knowledge and interests in the archaeology of the regions, he also contributed synchronisms in chronology, and associations in artifact typologies that have added greatly to our understanding of technological development, trade and commerce, and cultural stability and change in Egypt, Mesopotamia, and the entire Mediterranean world. His most basic single contribution, which has stood the test of time and remains our firm foundation for Levantine archaeology today, is the pottery typology and chronology that he developed in the 1920's and 1930's. We continue to build on that structure. We must also call attention to Albright's role in motivating and advising G. E. Wright's extension of that pottery chronology to include the Early Bronze period of the third millennium B.C.

Among other creative contributions is his holistic approach to ancient man and culture. All disciplines contribute information, and all information must fit harmoniously in a synthesis. Albright was a generalist, what we call today a "renaissance man," in controlling and integrating data from diverse disciplines. He taught us that we must respect, consider, and evaluate the research results from all disciplines as we form our syntheses. This approach is desperately needed not only today, but for the foreseeable future. Even though we are specialists with varying degrees of narrowness, we must seek to be generalists with varying degrees of breadth in our scholarship, lest the trees obscure our view of the forest.

Albright's autobiographical sketch, written in 1948 and later revised, contains the following evaluation of his own work and his basic view of the aims and methodologies of research; in a larger sense, they apply to all of us, and with this thoughtful summary I close:

"The subject of this essay [Albright] has always had the temper of a pioneer interested in surveying new routes and in breaking new ground. In the course of such a career many mistakes are bound to be made, and many hypotheses will have to be revised or discarded entirely. As time passes, a prudent investigator gradually learns to avoid certain types of research either as too subjective to yield safe results or as relatively unproductive. Above all he learns to value sound method, following approved logical principles of induction, deduction, and experiment. Yet "sound method" must not be permitted to become an obsession, for at that point the scholar is likely to become intellectually myopic and his work is likely to lose its heuristic value. Moreover, due respect for the traditions of true scholarship, aiming at truth and rejecting temptations to expose one's wares at the marketplace, should never be allowed to obscure the primary fact that all scholarly research which is worthy of the name must have a definite plan, a plan which will fit into the investigator's world view and enrich it at the same time that it is ennobled by it." (Albright 1964:310).

References

Albright, W. F.

1924   *Excavations and Results at Tell el-Fûl (Gibeah of Saul). Annual of the American Schools of Oriental Research* 4. New Haven.

1932   *The Excavation of Tell Beit Mirsim, I: The Pottery of the First Three Campaigns. Annual of the American Schools of Oriental Research* 12. New Haven.

1933   *The Excavation of Tell Beit Mirsim IA: The Bronze Age Pottery of the Fourth Campaign. Annual of the American Schools of Oriental Research* 13. New Haven.

1938   *The Excavation of Tell Beit Mirsim II: The Bronze Age. Annual of the American Schools of Oriental Research* 17. New Haven.

1940   *From the Stone Age to Christianity*: Monotheism and the Historical Process. Baltimore:Johns Hopkins Press.

1943   *The Excavation of Tell Beit Mirsim III: The Iron Age. Annual of the American Schools of Oriental Research*. New Haven.

1949   *The Archaeology of Palestine*. Harmondsworth:Penguin Books no. A199.

1964   *Archaeology, History, and Christian Humanism*. New York:McGraw-Hill.

Archaeological Institute of America

1968   *American Journal of Archaeology* 72:160.

Campbell, E. F. Jr. and J. M. Miller

1979   "W. F. Albright and Historical Reconstruction," *Biblical Archaeologist* 42:37-47.

Yadin, Y.

1969   "William Foxwell Albright," *Eretz Israel* 9:ix-xii. Jerusalem:Central Press.